OFFICERS and SOLDIERS

GW00385558

The FRENCH HUSSARS
1804-1815

Volume 2
1804-1812

First part. From the 1st to the 8th Regiment

André JOUINEAU

Translated from the French by Alan McKay

HISTOIRE & COLLECTIONS

Generalities

In the same way as the other cavalry corps of the Ancien Régime, the Hussars survived the Revolution, the Directoire and the Consulate without their uniforms changing substantially.

During the Empire, fashion changed and the look of the horseman evolved. The dolman and the pelisse became shorter, raising the Hussar's waist.

The shako

Little by little the mirliton cap changed into a cylindrical hat with a pennant, then into a taller, flattened-cone shaped shako, with a fixed visor. On the front there was a tricolour cockade with the white on the outside, a sign of belonging to the Nation. Napoleon did not care to modify this symbol because it recalled the fact that his army had its origins in the Republic. According to the 1806 dispositions, the shako had a new decoration: a lozenge-shaped plate made of tin or brass, stamped with an eagle and the number of the regiment. A leather chinstrap was added to the cord which was worn plaited on the front and the rear, and which was slipped round the neck and to prevent the rider from losing his hat when riding.

chinstrap was made of brass or tin scales fixed onto the leather strap going under the chin and was tied with laces. When dismounted, the trooper tucked the chinstrap up under the hat. Apart from holding the shako on, the jugular chinstrap also protected the rider from sabre blows. Finally a fob held the full dress plume which was usually black in place.

In marching or campaign dress, all the decorations were removed and either put in the portmanteau or stored at the depot. Only the company colour pompom, the plate and the cockade remained.

Hair

The cut was characteristic of the Light cavalry and the "dishevelled" fashion inherited from the Revolution. The hair was worn long so that it could be rolled up into a black ribbon. On the sides, the hair was arranged into "dog's ears" then plaited to form a lovelock, weighted at the tip. The whole was supposed to protect the rider from sabre blows. The young recruits had to let their hair grow for months before being able to have such a head of hair. Nevertheless at the beginning of the Empire, a number of

Generals asked for the hair to be worn short, mainly fc reasons of hygiene and upkeep, but the tradition died har among the Hussars and plaits and lovelocks lasted a lon time in spite of the edicts on the matter. To complete th Hussar's image, he had to sport a moustache, perpetua ting the "Houzard" traditions of the

Ancien Regime. For those among the young recruits wh could not grow this "virile" attribute, the tradition was mair tained by making a false moustache with a fire-blackene cork for parade days until the whiskers appeared.

The forage cap

This is cut like the Dragoons' with a turban and a pen nant the colour of the regimental distinctive. The pennan ended with a tassel the same colour as the plaits and the turban was decorated with white or yellow braid depen ding on the regiment.

The dolman

This item of clothing shows the Hungarian origin of this corps and was part of the prestige inherent in the Hussar uniform. On the front it was decorated with braid with three rows of eighteen – sometimes 13 or 15 – buttons which were changed to five in about 1812 in most of the regiments. The buttons were made of tin when the braid was white and brass when it was yellow; they were spherical when they were used for fastening something and semispherical when they were used for decoration.

The inside of the dolman was lined and stitched and the bottom had a leather band; the armholes were rather narrow and the bottoms of the sleeves were decorated with serrated facings ending in a point. They were generally the colour of the distinctive and decorated with flat braid. The collar was also decorated with flat braid; with time the collar got taller as the dolman got shorter at the waist.

The sash-belt

This was a woollen hank, nearly always crimson, with loops the same colour as the braid, fastening at the rear with a small cord whose extra length was wrapped around back towards the front.

The pelisse

Under the Ancien Regime, the pelisse was a rather long

acket which covered the small of the Hussar's back but lost this function with the change in fashion during the empire. It was decorated with braid and two or three rows of 15 – or sometimes 12 – buttons. It was lined with cloth and stitched, edged with black – for the most part—sheepskin fur.

It was narrow and was worn in one of two ways: either over the waistcoat (the dolman being packed away in the portmanteau), this manner being called *chaussée*; or slung over the left shoulder and held in place by its cord, or *jetée*.

The waistcoat

This was sleeveless, fastened with buttons, with or without a collar and sometimes decorated with braid. It could also have more trimmings or it could simply be buttoned up straight.

The breeches

These were typical of the Hussar's outfit and called Hungarian breeches. They had a fly, were tight-fitting and held up with braces. They were decorated with flat braid on the side seams and with two spades over the opening of the fly the same colour as the dolman braid. These spades were sometimes replaced by Hungarian knots or trefoils.

The boots

They were Hungarian-style and made of soft leather. The top of the boot was cut in the shape of a heart and decorated with a cord and a tassel the same colour as the braid. The boot was low and scarcely reached up to below the knee. Spurs were screwed into the heel.

The jacket

This often replaced all these rather sumptuous clothes during a campaign and in the cantonment. It was normally worn by the Hussars when they were campaigning. It was simply cut, fastening straight down with nine buttons, with shoulder flaps and a straight collar. The sleeves ended in pointed facings, often the same colour as the regimental distinctive colour, like the collar. There was a pocket with its flap tacked on either side.

The riding trousers

Also called charivari, they were ample and were worn over the Hungarian breeches to protect them. They were made to resist the weather and were reinforced with black sheepskin which was cut in different ways and shapes. The side openings had a cloth strip the same colour as the regi-

	1st Hussars	2nd Hussars	3rd Hussars	4th Hussars	5th Hussars	6th Hussars	7th Hussars	8th Hussars	9th Hussars	10th Hussars
PELISSE										
Background cloth	Dark sky blue	Brown	Argentine grey	Scarlet	White	Dark blue	Dark green	Dark green	Sky blue	Sky blue
Sheepskin lining	White	White	White	White	White	White	White	White	White	White
Laces	White	White	Crimson	Yellow	Lemon yell.	Yellow	Bright yell.	White	Yellow	White
Braid	White	White	Crimson	Yellow	Lemon yell.	Yellow	Bright yell.	White	Yellow	White
Buttons	Silver	Silver	Silver	Gold	Gold	Gold	Gold	Silver	Gold	Silver
DOLMAN										
Background cloth	Dark sky blue	Brown	Argentine grey	Dark blue	Sky blue	Scarlet	Dark green	Dark green	Scarlet	Sky blue
Collar	Dark sky blue	Brown	Argentine grey	Dark blue	Sky blue	Dark blue	Scarlet	Scarlet	Sky blue	Scarlet
Facings	Scarlet	Sky blue	Crimson	Scarlet	White	Dark blue	Scarlet	Scarlet	Sky blue	Scarlet
Braid	White	White	Crimson	Yellow	Lemon yell.	Yellow	Bright yell.	White	Yellow	White
Buttons	Silver	Silver	Silver	Gold	Gold	Gold	Gold	Silver	Gold	Silver
WAISTCOAT	Dark sky blue	Sky blue	Argentine grey	Scarlet	Scarlet	Scarlet	Scarlet	Scarlet	Sky blue	Scarlet
BREECHES	Dark sky blue	Sky blue	Argentine grey	Dark blue	Sky blue	Dark blue	Scarlet	Scarlet	Sky blue	Sky blue
BARREL SASH										
Cord	Crimson	Crimson	Crimson	Crimson	Crimson	Crimson	Crimson	Crimson	Crimson	Crimson
Barrel	White	White	White	Yellow	Lemon yell.	Yellow	Bright yell.	White	Yellow	White
SHAKO										
Body	Black	Black	Black	Black	Sky blue	Black	Black	Black	Black	Black
Plume	Black	Black	Black	Black	White	Black	Black	Black	Black	Scarlet
Top of the plume	Black	Black	Black	Black	White	Scarlet	Black	Scarlet	White	Black
Cord and tassel	White	White	Crimson	Yellow	none	Yellow	Bright yell.	White	Yellow	White
Metal part of the chinstrap	Silver	Silver	Silver	Gold	Gold	Gold	Gold	Silver	Gold	Silver

mental distinctive and were fastened with buttons down the whole length of the leg. The opening was wide. There was a strap under the arch of the foot. When there were any, the pockets were on the front and were of different shapes.

Canvas trousers

Made of natural-coloured canvas, these were ample and were worn as the stable or cantonment uniform with the jacket. They were however worn in Spain because of the summer heat.

The coat

This was green and comprised a big hood which covered the headdress. It was sufficiently ample to cover the rider, the rear part of the saddle and the rear of the horse. When it was not used it was rolled up in front of the saddle, or worn saltire-wise during battle as extra protection for the Hussar from sabre blows.

The equipment

This had scarcely changed since the 1786 rules. The cartridge-case belt was made of white buffalo hide. It ended with a buckle and a brass carrier. The cartridge box was slightly smaller since Louis XVI's Hussars. The musketoon-holder belt was attached by means of a copper button. A movable steel hook enabled the rider to hold his musketoon whilst riding. The belt was fitted with two loops to carry the sabre and three straps for the sabretache; everything was adjusted by means of buckles. The belt was fastened by means of a brass buckle.

The sabretache

This symbol of the Hussar uniform was not exactly very useful except for carrying small documents or miscellaneous items. The slightly curved shape had changed a little since the Ancien Regime. The sabretache was made of leather with an embroidered and braided cloth flap top. The Republican symbols were replaced by the Imperial Eagle in certain regiments. It systematically bore the number of the regiment, crowned or surrounded by laurel leaves. This fragile object was often put inside a leather cover for protection against the weather. This cover also often bore the number of the regiment painted on it or cut out of brass or tin. The embroidered sabretaches gave way progressively to the black leather models, merely decorated with the number of the regiment, an eagle or a copper element with the regimental number cut out.

Weapons

There were two sorts: firearms and the rest. The main cavalry weapon was the curved Light Cavalry sabre already in use during the Ancien Regime with a single guard and a brass scabbard; it was replaced during the Empire by a sabre with a steel scabbard and three brass guards. On the hilt there was a leather thong which held the sabre to the man's wrist. At the beginning of the Empire the firearms consisted of the 1786-model musketoon replaced gradually by the An XI model. It could be fitted with a bayonet but this was not used very much as it was thought to be cumbersome and of no great utility. Its scabbard was attached between the first and second buckles on the belt. In theory the Hussar was equipped with a pair of pistols but this was reduced to one because of the lack of firearms.

During campaigns broken weapons were not replaced immediately and it was not rare to see certain horsemen armed with Prussian Light Cavalry sabres and Austrian musketoons.

Saddles

These were especially for the Light Cavalry. They consisted of a wooden tree onto which a heavy piece of leather was sewn; the whole was placed on a folded-over blanket in order not to harm the horse's back and was held on to the horse by means of the girth belt. In front of the saddle there was a pair of holsters for the pistols; the coat was often rolled over these. The saddle was covered with a sheepskin "wolf's teeth"-scalloped shabrack. It was smaller since the Ancien Regime. There was a slit in the rear of the shabrack for the cantle flap, as well as the straps for attaching the portmanteau. Another slit was made in the front on the right for the strap holding the musketoon in place.

The portmanteau was attached on the rear and was used as a haversack for the rider. It contained the other parts of his uniform, his personal objects, the oat bag for the horse and its brush. It was cylindrical, made of cloth the same colour as the regiment, lined with strong natural-coloured canvas and fastened on with three buckles. The ends were decorated with flat braid and sometimes with the regimental number cut from cloth.

All the leather straps were black. The harness was Hungarian-style with steel buckles and brass ornaments. The snaffle reins ended with a whip. The bits were made of steel and decorated with a brass stud stamped with the symbol of the arm or the number of the regiment.

Full Parade Dress

The Elite Company

This was created in 1802 and had the rank of the 1st Company in the 1st Squadron. The horsemen were differentiated by wearing the colback and a red plume.

The rest was in all points identical to all the other Hussars in the other companies.

Trooper from the 4th Hussars in about 1810.

Hussar from the 7th Regiment in about 1810, mounted and on foot, rear view. The musketoon is carried on its belt. The sabre is the model in use at the beginning of the Empire, and the scabbard is the steel model.

Clothing Items

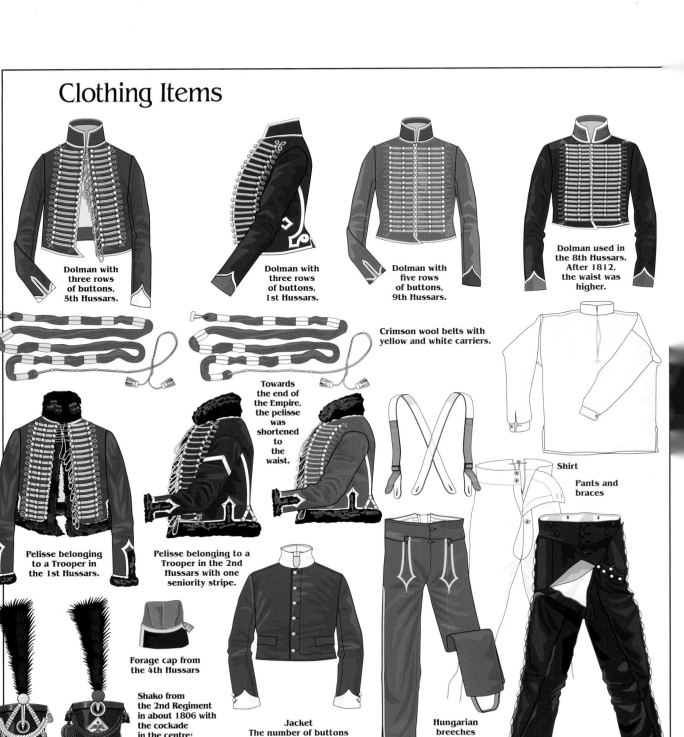

Dolman with three rows of buttons, 5th Hussars.

Dolman with three rows of buttons, 1st Hussars.

Dolman with five rows of buttons, 9th Hussars.

Dolman used in the 8th Hussars. After 1812, the waist was higher.

Crimson wool belts with yellow and white carriers.

Towards the end of the Empire, the pelisse was shortened to the waist.

Shirt

Pants and braces

Pelisse belonging to a Trooper in the 1st Hussars.

Pelisse belonging to a Trooper in the 2nd Hussars with one seniority stripe.

Forage cap from the 4th Hussars

Shako from the 2nd Regiment in about 1806 with the cockade in the centre; a shako from the 8th Hussars towards 1811 with the lozenge-shaped plate.

Jacket
The number of buttons varied, the facings were pointed although some were in the shape of a sheaf.

Hungarian breeches

Riding trousers

8

The Equipment

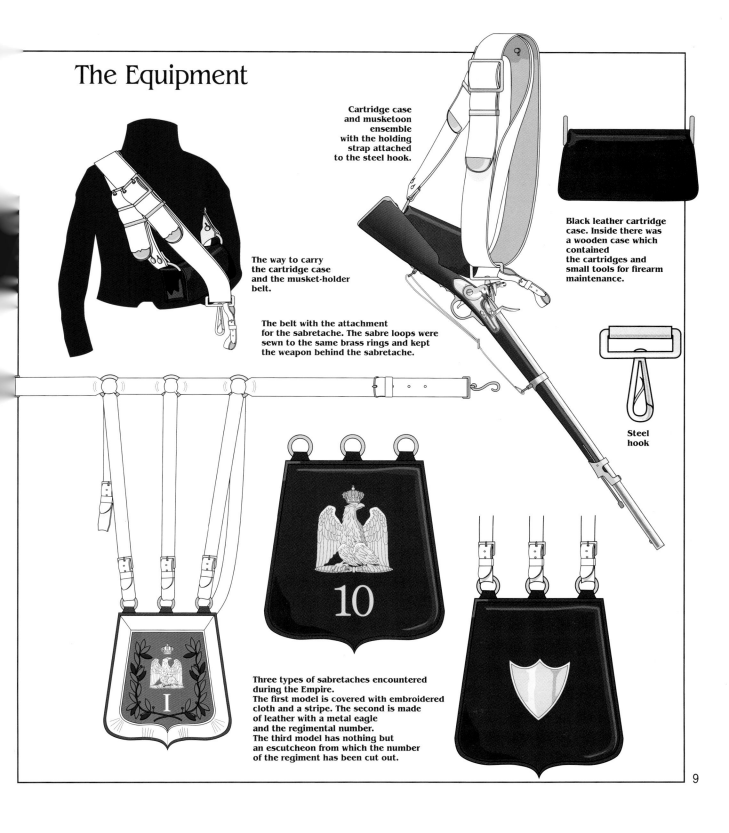

Cartridge case and musketoon ensemble with the holding strap attached to the steel hook.

The way to carry the cartridge case and the musket-holder belt.

The belt with the attachment for the sabretache. The sabre loops were sewn to the same brass rings and kept the weapon behind the sabretache.

Black leather cartridge case. Inside there was a wooden case which contained the cartridges and small tools for firearm maintenance.

Steel hook

10

I

Three types of sabretaches encountered during the Empire.
The first model is covered with embroidered cloth and a stripe. The second is made of leather with a metal eagle and the regimental number.
The third model has nothing but an escutcheon from which the number of the regiment has been cut out.

Weapons

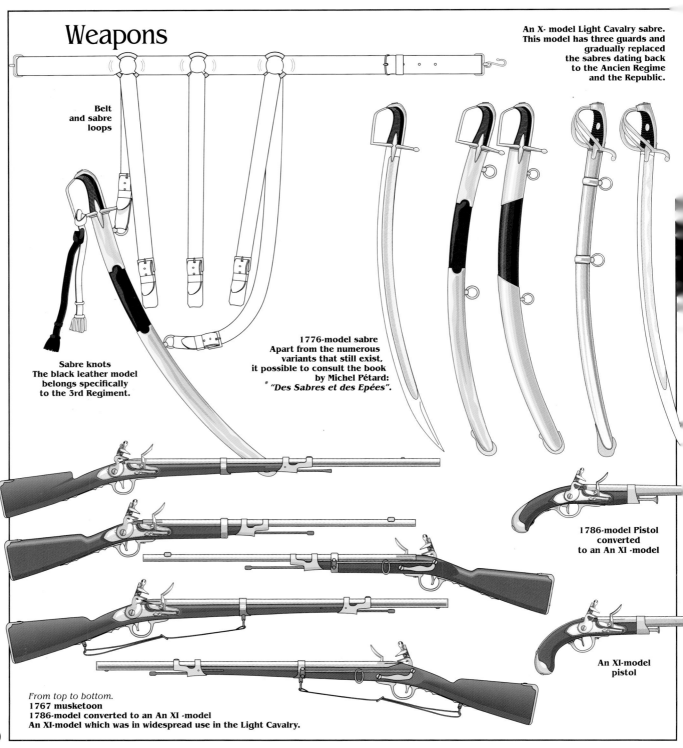

Belt
and sabre
loops

An X- model Light Cavalry sabre.
This model has three guards and
gradually replaced
the sabres dating back
to the Ancien Regime
and the Republic.

Sabre knots
The black leather model
belongs specifically
to the 3rd Regiment.

1776-model sabre
Apart from the numerous
variants that still exist,
it possible to consult the book
by Michel Pétard:
"Des Sabres et des Epées".

1786-model Pistol
converted
to an An XI -model

An XI-model
pistol

From top to bottom.
1767 musketoon
1786-model converted to an An XI -model
An XI-model which was in widespread use in the Light Cavalry.

10

Saddles

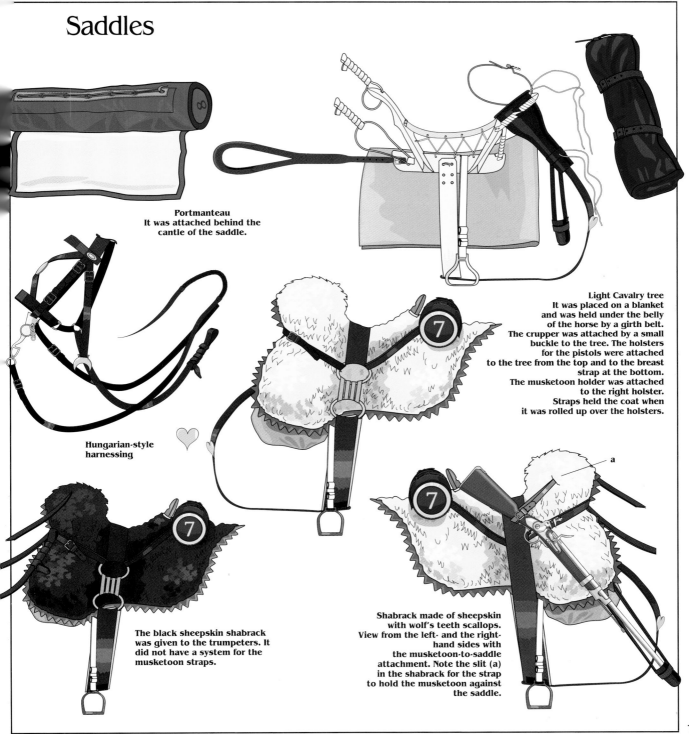

Portmanteau
It was attached behind the cantle of the saddle.

Hungarian-style harnessing

Light Cavalry tree
It was placed on a blanket and was held under the belly of the horse by a girth belt. The crupper was attached by a small buckle to the tree. The holsters for the pistols were attached to the tree from the top and to the breast strap at the bottom. The musketoon holder was attached to the right holster. Straps held the coat when it was rolled up over the holsters.

The black sheepskin shabrack was given to the trumpeters. It did not have a system for the musketoon straps.

Shabrack made of sheepskin with wolf's teeth scallops. View from the left- and the right-hand sides with the musketoon-to-saddle attachment. Note the slit (a) in the shabrack for the strap to hold the musketoon against the saddle.

The distinctives

Trooper
from the
1st Hussar Regiment

Trooper
from the
2nd Hussar Regiment

Trooper
from the
3rd Hussar Regiment

Trooper
from the 4th
Hussar Regiment

Trooper
from the 5th
Hussar Regiment

The distinctives

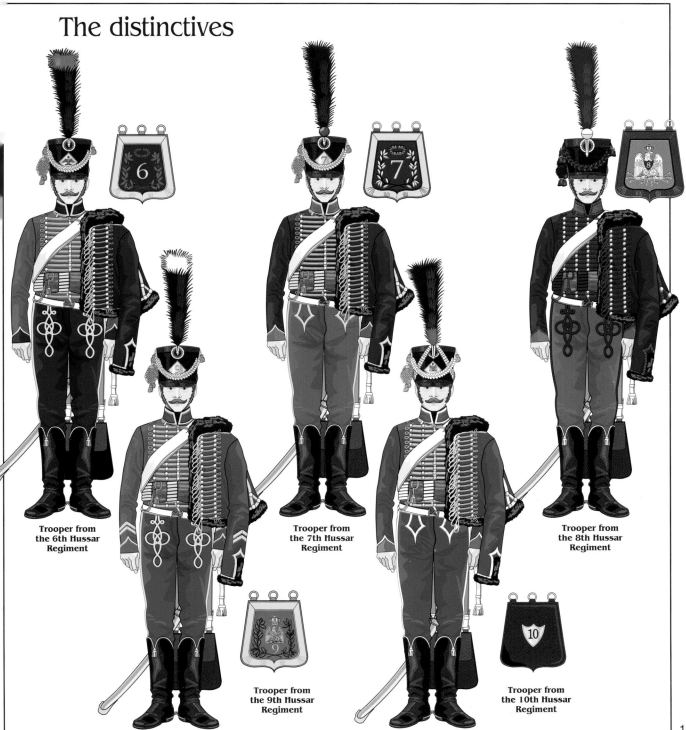

Trooper from
the 6th Hussar
Regiment

Trooper from
the 7th Hussar
Regiment

Trooper from
the 8th Hussar
Regiment

Trooper from
the 9th Hussar
Regiment

Trooper from
the 10th Hussar
Regiment

The Non-Commissioned Officers

Adjudant from the 2nd Hussars

The Adjudant Sous-Officier is wearing
a very similar uniform to that
of the officers; he has kept however
the troopers' braid and has three stripes
on the sleeve of the dolman
and the pelisse.
The shako has an upper stripe
in silver or gold thread with
a red zigzag going through it.
In going-out dress, he wore
a frock coat with a gold or silver
mixed, with the red epaulette
of his rank.

The stripes of rank worn
on the dolman and the pelisse
are made of gold or silver thread
depending on the metal
of the button.

The NCOs
from Maréchal-des-Logis
upwards were not armed
with a musketoon.
Certain NCOs wore
a pelisse edged with fox fur
rather than black sheepskin.

**Maréchal-des-Logis
in the 5th Hussars**

**Maréchal-des-Logis
from the Elite
Company
of the 9th Hussars**

Ranks, from left to right:
- Trooper with one seniority stripe
- Brigadier
- Brigadier-Fourrier
- Maréchal-des-Logis with one seniority
stripe
- Maréchal-des-Logis Chef
- Adjudant
Depending on the colour of the button,
the stripes were yellow and gold.

14

The Officers

They wore the same uniform as the soldiers but it was tailored from finer cloth. All the trimmings were gold or silver depending on the buttons. The ranks were worn above the dolman facings, on the pelisse sleeves and on the front of the breeches. The pelisses were edged with fur. Depending on how wealthy the officer was the trimmings were more or less luxurious, with more Russian braid and brilliant ornamentation. In full dress, the officer's shabrack was made of panther-skin with wolf's teeth scallops and edged with silver or gold together with more or less sumptuous harnesses; or it was made of embroidered cloth with gold or silver braid for the less wealthy.

Officer from the 2nd Hussars wearing social dress

Officer from the 2nd Hussars wearing a frock coat

Lieutenant from the 1st Hussars in summer dress

Lieutenant from the 7th Hussars in full dress

Officer from the 5th Hussars in town dress

Clothing Items

Woollen belts which had silver or gold thread carriers depending on the colour of the button.

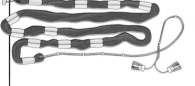

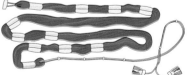

Dolman belonging to a Lieutenant from the 7th Hussars

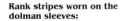

Rank stripes worn on the dolman sleeves:
- Sub-Lieutenant
- Lieutenant
- Captain
- Squadron Commander
- Lieutenant-Colonel or Major
- Colonel

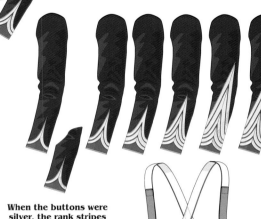

Half-bell buttons
As on the dolman, the half-bell buttons were sewn onto the braid. Bell buttons were used for fastening.

When the buttons were silver, the rank stripes were also silver.

Rank stripes for the Hungarian breeches

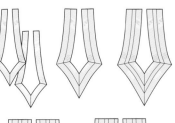

Forage cap
For senior officers, there was a double stripe.

Shirt

Waistcoat
It was always sleeveless, with or without a collar.

The flat braid on the side seam was doubled for the senior officers.

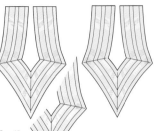

Rank stripes for the Major when the buttons were gold (top) or silver (bottom).

Lieutenant's Hungarian breeches

Equipment, Town dress

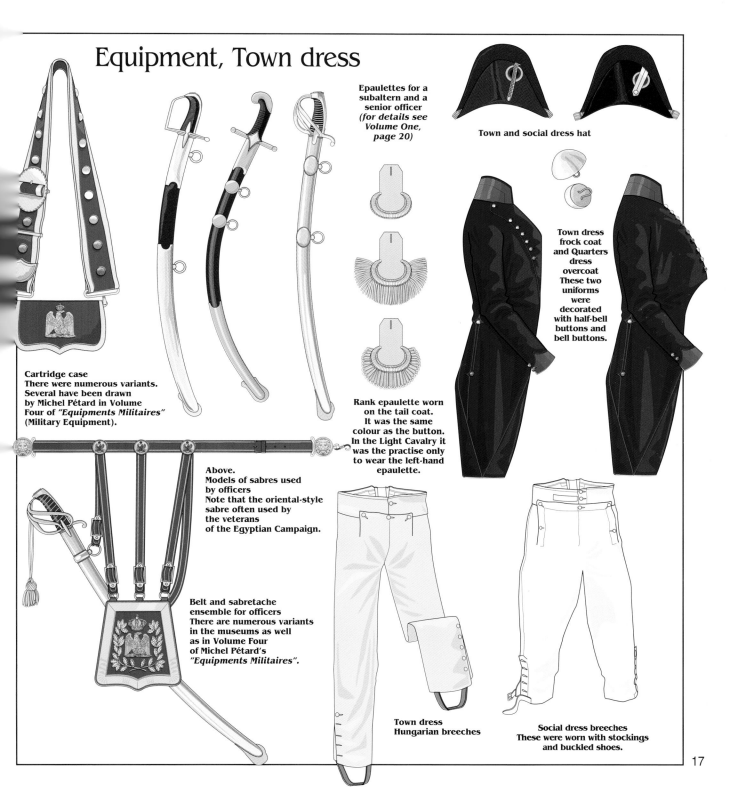

Epaulettes for a subaltern and a senior officer *(for details see Volume One, page 20)*

Town and social dress hat

Town dress frock coat and Quarters dress overcoat These two uniforms were decorated with half-bell buttons and bell buttons.

Cartridge case
There were numerous variants. Several have been drawn by Michel Pétard in Volume Four of *"Equipments Militaires"* (Military Equipment).

Rank epaulette worn on the tail coat. It was the same colour as the button. In the Light Cavalry it was the practise only to wear the left-hand epaulette.

Above.
Models of sabres used by officers
Note that the oriental-style sabre often used by the veterans of the Egyptian Campaign.

Belt and sabretache ensemble for officers
There are numerous variants in the museums as well as in Volume Four of Michel Pétard's *"Equipments Militaires"*.

Town dress Hungarian breeches

Social dress breeches
These were worn with stockings and buckled shoes.

Saddles

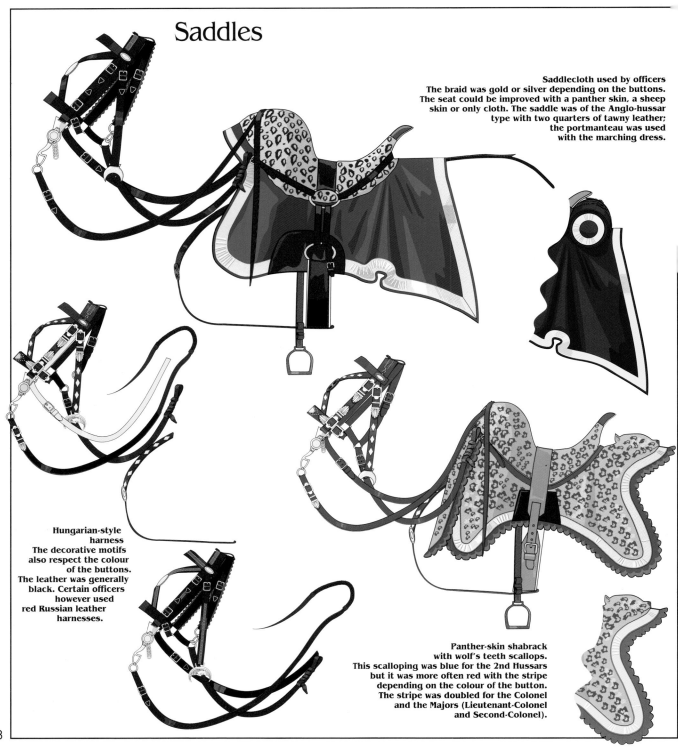

Saddlecloth used by officers
The braid was gold or silver depending on the buttons.
The seat could be improved with a panther skin, a sheep
skin or only cloth. The saddle was of the Anglo-hussar
type with two quarters of tawny leather;
the portmanteau was used
with the marching dress.

Hungarian-style harness
The decorative motifs
also respect the colour
of the buttons.
The leather was generally
black. Certain officers
however used
red Russian leather
harnesses.

Panther-skin shabrack
with wolf's teeth scallops.
This scalloping was blue for the 2nd Hussars
but it was more often red with the stripe
depending on the colour of the button.
The stripe was doubled for the Colonel
and the Majors (Lieutenant-Colonel
and Second-Colonel).

The 1st Hussar Regiment
(ex-Bercheny)

The 1st Regiment is the descendant of the *Bercheny Hussars* of the Ancien Regime. Its distinctive colour was royal blue, a name which disappeared with the Revolution but which corresponds to a dark sky blue. We cannot be more precise about the colour because as the colours were made by craftsmen, they resisted exposure to the sun and the weather rather badly; this created quite different shades of colours from one horseman to another.

At the beginning of the Empire, the Hussars still wore the cylindrical shako inherited from the Consular period with a detachable visor. It was gradually replaced by the 1806 model with a pair of scale chinstraps and a cockade and its braid. It was only towards 1807-1808 that the lozenge plate stamped with the regimental number appeared. It was replaced by an 1810-model number plate then by an eagle on a base.

The dolman had three rows of buttons and this increased to five in around 1807.

The Hungarian breeches were the same shade as the dolman. In about 1808, they became scarlet for the whole the regiment. This modification corresponds to the period when the 10th Hussar Regiment was created and adopted the same distinctive colours but with a lighter shade, with the same braid and the same buttons.

Band and trumpeters

The 1st Regiment had a band created under the Consulate on 6 April 1802. The strength of the band is not known because these units were not required by the regulations and were kept up at the expense of the regiment by the officer corps. On the whole, the musicians wore the trumpeter's uniform and the bandmaster was an NCO. Some uniforms have come down to us by means of the Alsatian Collections: thus we know of a timpanist, an oboist and a bandmaster.

The trumpeter's job was to transmit orders given by the officers to the troopers. So there was a different sound for each order or movement which the horsemen had to make. Learning the different sounds was done during training and in the field. Although he had to be heard the trumpeter also had to be seen; this is why in the cavalry the colours of the trumpeter's uniform were the reverse of the troopers' uniform. This practise has been confirmed in most cases.

During the Empire however, it is possible to come across instances of trumpeters being dressed differently depending on the wishes of the regiment's colonel, on regimental tradition or simply on the circumstances of the moment.

For the saddle, the shabrack was normally made of black sheepskin. Here again one can come across variants such as a saddlecloth made of cloth with or without a seat made of sheepskin, or more simply, just the same shabrack as the troopers. On the other hand, the remount was always made on grey horses. Finally the trumpeter was armed with a sabre and a pair of pistols, but no musketoon and therefore he did not wear a musketoon-holder belt.

Officers

The officers were dressed like the troopers but heir uniforms were tailored from finer cloth and a silver stripe replaced the white one of the troopers. An engraving by A. Martinet shows an officer from the Elite Company wearing a particularly sumptuous uniform; on the other hand, N. Hoffmann shows officers at the beginning of the Empire wearing a uniform still greatly influenced by the Ancien Regime.

In the middle of the Empire, the officers frequently wore colbacks although these were normally reserved for the Elite Company. However to preserve these especially expensive and luxurious uniforms the campaigning officer would wear much a simpler one.

Four eagles with the 1804-model standard were given to the regiment. Only the standard belonging to the 3rd Squadron, captured by the Allies in Paris in 1815, was kept in the Berlin Museum.

The 1st Hussars

The colours of the company pompoms have been established from a plate by Rigo for the first column and by H. Malibran for the second. Variations existed and could have existed alongside each other. As the regiments were rarely at full strength some companies were sometimes not formed.

1. 1st Company
2. 5th Company
3. 2nd Company
4. 6th Company
5. 3rd Company
6. 7th Company
7. 4th Company
8. 8th Company

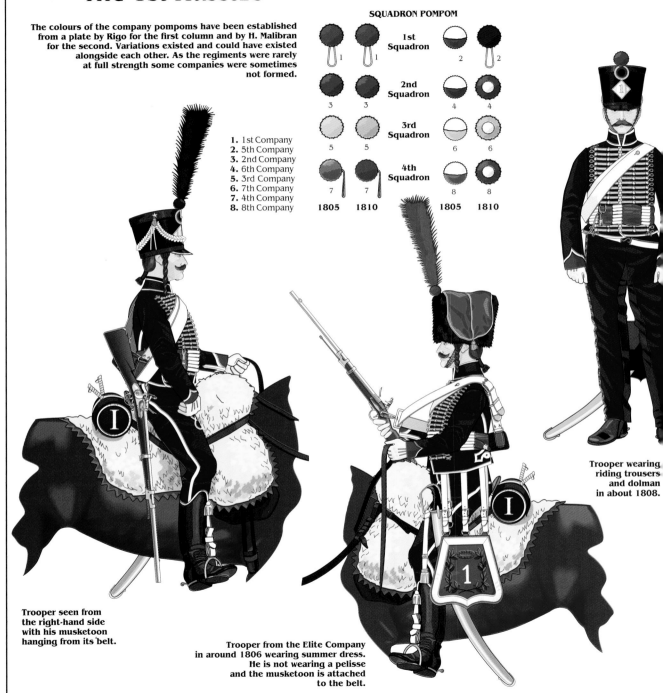

SQUADRON POMPOM

1	1	**1st Squadron**	2	2
3	3	**2nd Squadron**	4	4
5	5	**3rd Squadron**	6	6
7	7	**4th Squadron**	8	8
1805	1810		1805	1810

Trooper seen from the right-hand side with his musketoon hanging from its belt.

Trooper from the Elite Company in around 1806 wearing summer dress. He is not wearing a pelisse and the musketoon is attached to the belt.

Trooper wearing riding trousers and dolman in about 1808.

20

The 1st Hussars: the Troopers

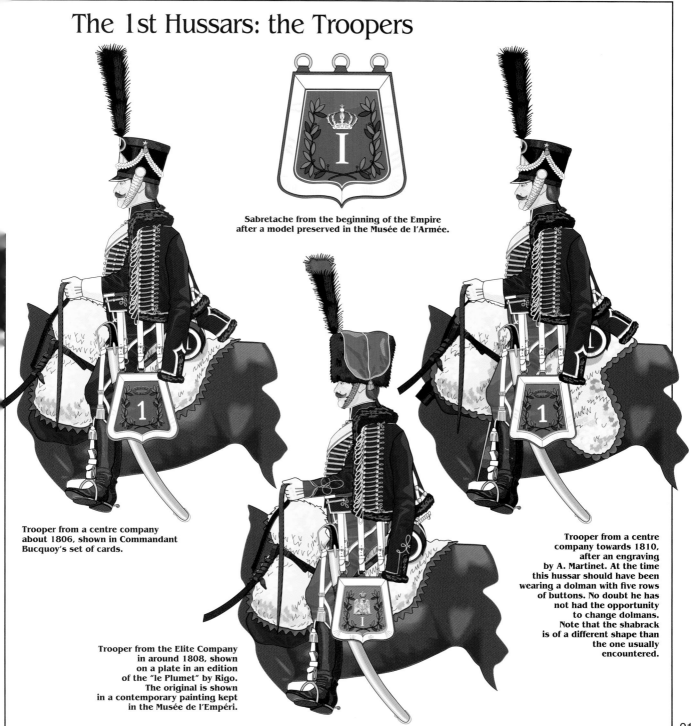

Sabretache from the beginning of the Empire
after a model preserved in the Musée de l'Armée.

Trooper from a centre company
about 1806, shown in Commandant
Bucquoy's set of cards.

Trooper from the Elite Company
in around 1808, shown
on a plate in an edition
of the "le Plumet" by Rigo.
The original is shown
in a contemporary painting kept
in the Musée de l'Empéri.

Trooper from a centre
company towards 1810,
after an engraving
by A. Martinet. At the time
this hussar should have been
wearing a dolman with five rows
of buttons. No doubt he has
not had the opportunity
to change dolmans.
Note that the shabrack
is of a different shape than
the one usually
encountered.

The 1st Hussars: the Troopers

**Trooper's uniform worn
in Spain towards 1809.**

**The hussar seems to be wearing riding
breeches made from canvas. This uniform
has been taken from Commandant
Bucquoy's set off cards.**

**Hussar wearing
a pelisse
and riding trousers
in about 1807.**

**Campaign dress towards
the middle of the Empire.
This was the uniform
most commonly worn
by the Hussars when
campaigning, thus
protecting the Hungarian-
style uniform from
the weather.
Drawing by P. Benigni.**

**Sapper from the regiment
according to the Alsatian
Collections.**

**We know of a picture of another
sapper in the 3rd Regiment.
His Light Cavalry sabre with
the hilt of a sapper's sabre does
however seem strange.**

The 1st Hussars: the Brigadiers

Brigadier wearing training uniform according to a drawing by P. Benigni.

THE SABRETACHES

There were six types of sabretache worn by the Hussars during this period.

— **The first** could be called the *"Consular type"* and was from 1801 to 1807. Its decoration consisted of a number surmounted by a civic crown and surrounded by two branches of leaves.

— **The second type** (1804-1812) still had a number with two branches of leaves but was surmounted by the Imperial Crown.

— **The third** type which can be identified was used from 1804 to 1812 and bore the eagle surrounded – or not - by two branches of leaves and surmounted with the Imperial Crown. The sabretache was covered with cloth.

— **The fourth,** just like the fifth, appeared at the end of our period. The flap was made of leather and was decorated with a number or an escutcheon.

— **The fifth** (seen especially between 1809 and 1812) was made of leather and had a crowned eagle.

— **The 1812** model had a leather flap and a crowned eagle surmounting the number of the regiment. This sabretache was the first one which was perfectly regulated by Bardin.

After Bertrand Malvaux in "la Cavalerie Légère du Premier Empire."

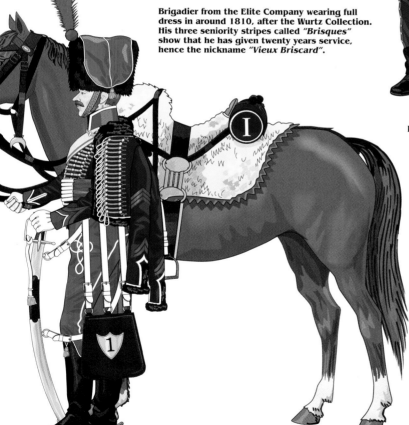

Brigadier from the Elite Company wearing full dress in around 1810, after the Wurtz Collection. His three seniority stripes called *"Brisques"* show that he has given twenty years service, hence the nickname *"Vieux Briscard"*.

Brigadier-Fourrier in full dress according to V. Huen in around 1812. Note that the Brigadier-Fourrier is an NCO because of his job.

The 1st Hussars: the NCOs

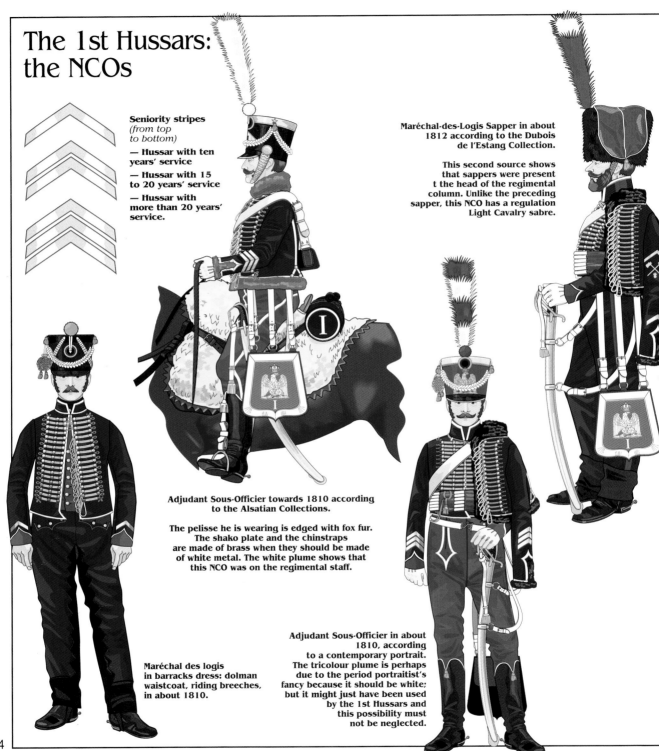

Seniority stripes
(from top to bottom)

— Hussar with ten years' service

— Hussar with 15 to 20 years' service

— Hussar with more than 20 years' service.

Maréchal-des-Logis Sapper in about 1812 according to the Dubois de l'Estang Collection.

This second source shows that sappers were present t the head of the regimental column. Unlike the preceding sapper, this NCO has a regulation Light Cavalry sabre.

Adjudant Sous-Officier towards 1810 according to the Alsatian Collections.

The pelisse he is wearing is edged with fox fur. The shako plate and the chinstraps are made of brass when they should be made of white metal. The white plume shows that this NCO was on the regimental staff.

Maréchal des logis in barracks dress: dolman waistcoat, riding breeches, in about 1810.

Adjudant Sous-Officier in about 1810, according to a contemporary portrait. The tricolour plume is perhaps due to the period portraitist's fancy because it should be white; but it might just have been used by the 1st Hussars and this possibility must not be neglected.

24

The 1st Hussars: the Trumpeters

Trumpeter from the ordinary company towards 1807.

Trumpeter from the ordinary company towards 1807. He is wearing the pelisse.

Trumpeter from the Elite Company in about 1808.

Trumpeter from the Elite Company in full parade dress in about 1809 according to a plate by Rigo in "le Plumet".

Detail of a trumpeeter's Sabretache (Elite Company).

The 1st Hussars: the Trumpeters

Brigadier Trumpeter according to the Alsatian Collections in about 1810. The stripes of rank are the reverse colour of the troopers'.

THE SABRETACHES *(continued)*

During the whole period, the sabretache had a curved base with a more or less sharp angle. Although the material and the way it was made changed over the years, the basic materials used for the sabretache were still the same: calf skin, sheepskin, cloth, wool or finer leather for the officers.

Its size did not change very much and the shape went from almost square to the more classic shape of 1812.

The sabretache measured thus between 12 and 13-inches high and 12-inches wide, reducing to 8-inches depending on the periods. The 1812 regulation model measured 12-inches high, 8-inches wide with a 12-inch base.

After Bertrand Malvaux in "la Cavalerie Légère du Premier Empire."

Trumpeter in about 1806 according to a drawing by P.A. Leroux.

Trumpeter from the Elite Company in about 1810 in the Dubois de l'Estang Collection.

The 1st Hussars: the Band

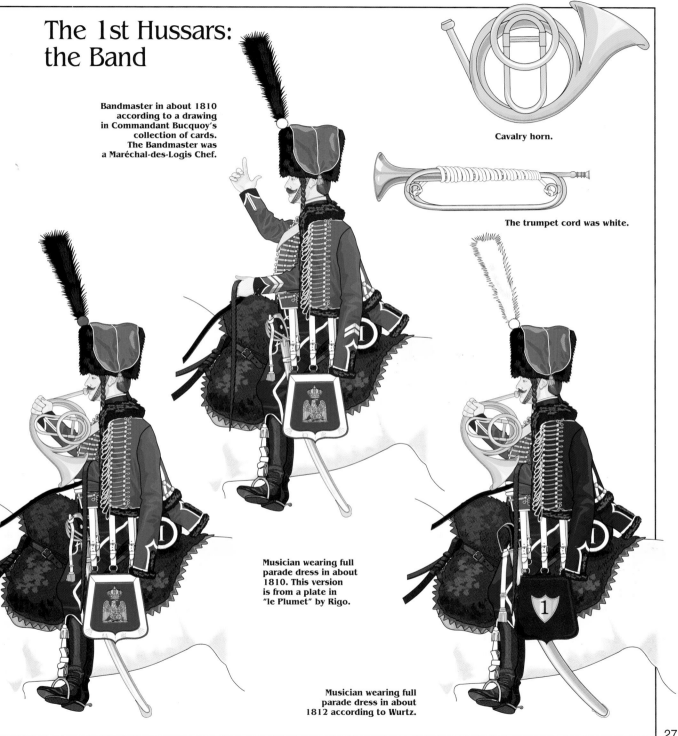

Bandmaster in about 1810 according to a drawing in Commandant Bucquoy's collection of cards. The Bandmaster was a Maréchal-des-Logis Chef.

Cavalry horn.

The trumpet cord was white.

Musician wearing full parade dress in about 1810. This version is from a plate in "le Plumet" by Rigo.

Musician wearing full parade dress in about 1812 according to Wurtz.

27

The 1st Hussars: the Officers

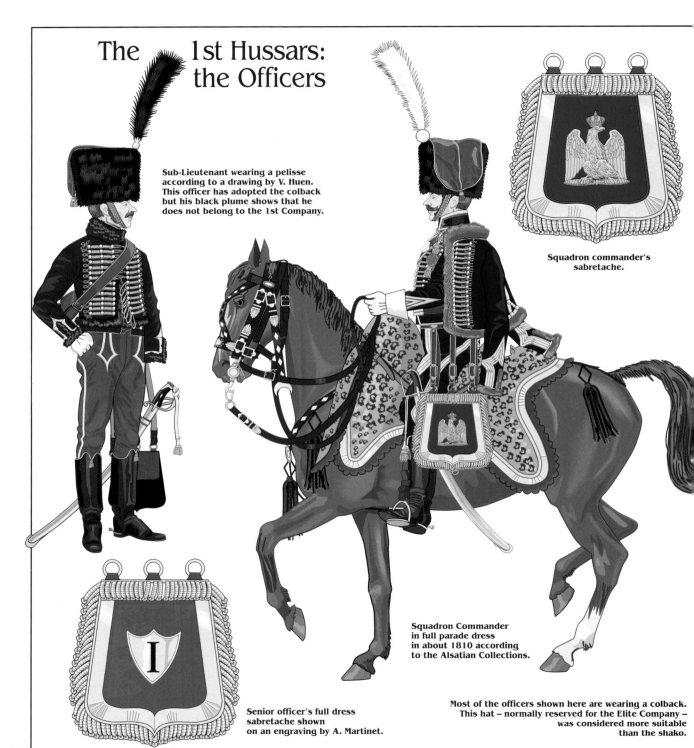

Sub-Lieutenant wearing a pelisse according to a drawing by V. Huen. This officer has adopted the colback but his black plume shows that he does not belong to the 1st Company.

Squadron commander's sabretache.

Squadron Commander in full parade dress in about 1810 according to the Alsatian Collections.

Senior officer's full dress sabretache shown on an engraving by A. Martinet.

Most of the officers shown here are wearing a colback. This hat – normally reserved for the Elite Company – was considered more suitable than the shako.

The 1st Hussars: the Officers

Sub-Lieutenant in Spain in about 1812.
The Anglo-hussar saddle does not have its saddlecloth. The officer is wearing rather wide trousers over his boots. Drawing by P. Benigni.

Officer wearing town dress in winter, according to Commandant Bucquoy's collections.

Lieutenant from the Elite Company in around 1812, after the Wurtz Collection.

Officer wearing social dress according to Commandant Bucquoy's collections.

The 2nd Hussar Regiment
(ex-Chamborant)

Whilst in command of the 2nd Hussar Regiment at the beginning of the Empire, Colonel Barbier left us a precious record of uniforms, precious because of the care he showed for detail in his gouaches. Because he was a good witness of his period he was able to paint the different uniforms worn by the officers and the men in his regiment.

The 2nd Hussars, formerly the *Chamborant Regiment* during the Ancien Regime, used brown and sky blue as its distinctives. The shades of the brown are known thanks to Colonel Barbier's gouaches and the items of uniforms preserved in the Musée de l'Armée and the Musée de l'Empéri (the Musée de l'Armée is in Paris whereas the Musée de l'Empéri is in Salon de Provence).

Uniforms

The uniform at the beginning of the Empire is the same as the one used during the Consulate. The slightly flattened-cone-shaped shako replaced the cylindrical shako. The headdress has no plate and is decorated with a cockade whose centre is blue with red on the outside, held in place by a white loop and a tin button.

The shako plate was only generalised in 1808 within the regiment; the lozenge plates however and those with an eagle existed side by side for some time afterwards.

The dolman had three rows of buttons for some time whereas the other regiments had five perhaps because there was a tradition which tended to distinguish this regiment from the others.

At the beginning of the Empire, some Hussars still wore sabretaches which dated back to the Republic. In so far as they did not display republican symbols, one can suppose that they were kept until they wore out.

In Spain, the troopers adapted themselves to the hot climate of the Sierra by wearing a lighter uniform comprising the jacket and breeches made of canvas cloth or stable breeches used as riding breeches.

In 1804, the trumpeters wore the same colours as the troopers. They could be distinguished afterwards first by the fact that they wore a uniform using a French-style coat decorated with braid, then finally by the uniform with the colours reversed.

Unlike for the 1st Regiment, there were no Sappers or Musicians known to have been marching at the head of the column.

The officers were like the troopers but with silver buttons and trimmings. However, when the regiment was in Spain, officers' uniforms seemed to be more extravagant especially one belonging to a senior officer who barely respected the regimental distinctives as his sky blue breeches were replaced by brown Hungarian-style ones.

Note that a lot of cavalry uniforms during the campaign in Spain were tailored from brown cloth, but it must not be thought that this was necessarily widespread.

In full parade dress, the officers used panther-skin shabracks; however, pictures made in Spain or even in Germany, show saddlecloths made of cloth or sheepskin festooned with sky blue.

This would tend to show that the panther-skin was too fragile and too expensive to be used when campaigning.

The HUSSAR REGIMENT in 1803

The Hussar Regiments towards 1803 comprised two-company squadrons and a headquarters.

The **Headquarters** comprised:
— 1 Brigade Commander
— 3 Squadron Commanders
— 2 Adjudant-Majors
— 1 Quarter-Master-Paymaster
— 1 Surgeon-Major
— 2 Adjudant NCOs
— 1 Veterinary officer
— 1 Trumpet-Major
— 1 Blacksmith
— 1 Master-Craftsman Saddler
— 1 Master-Craftsman Tailor
— 1 Master-Craftsman Cobbler

1 Master-Craftsman Armourer and few children of the regiment

The strength of the regiment was split up among the eight **companies** thus:
— 1 Captain
— 1 Lieutenant
— 2 Second-lieutenants
— 1 *Maréchal des Logis Chef*
— 4 *Maréchals des Logis*
— 1 *Brigadier-Fourrier*
— 8 *Brigadiers*
— 2 Trumpeters
— 80 Hussars

These figures were given for the 2nd Hussars in 1803.

The 2nd Hussars: the Troopers

Cavalryman wearing a bivouac coat, on the eve of the Battle of Austerlitz according to a gouache by Colonel Barbier.

Trooper wearing going-out dress, according to full length portrait of the period.

Trooper wearing parade dress towards 1810.

Trooper wearing parade dress according to the set of engravings by A. Martinet.

Trooper wearing parade dress towards 1807, according to a German engraving of the time. The shako does not have a plate yet.

The 2nd Hussars: the Troopers

Trooper wearing going-out dress in about 1807, by the "Burger of Hamburg".

Trooper's sabretaches, in about 1806.

Trooper wearing campaign dress in 1805-1807 drawn by Colonel Barbier.

Trooper wearing campaign dress towards 1805-1807 after the "Otto Manuscript". Note the black and white mixed braid on the pelisse, the shako chinstrap made of brass and the sabretache emblem.

Trooper wearing a pelisse and breeches in 1807.

The 2nd Hussars: the Troopers

Trooper around 1810 wearing parade dress, according to the Alsatian Collections. It does not differ from that given by A. Martinet except for the background of the sabretache and the shako pompom – which should be another colour since red was attributed to the Elite Company— as well as the facings of the dolman which are brown when they should be sky blue.

Trooper towards 1807 in campaign dress, according to a German engraving. The sabretache uses a brass emblem as shown on an engraving from the "Otto Manuscript" which dates back to the same period.

Trooper in about 1808 wearing campaign dress in Spain. He is wearing a jacket and riding breeches made from canvas cloth in order to be better adapted to the country's climate. The Hussar's dress loses in splendour what it gains in practicality.

Imperial Eagles for the 2nd hussars

Until 1814, each squadron's standard was carried by an NCO, designated by the Colonel and not on his staff.

For taking part in the Battle of Austerlitz, the 2nd Hussars were awarded two gold crowns for their eagles by the City of Paris. It was only on 26 September 1808 when the regiment returned to France on its way to Spain that it received these two crowns which thereafter decorated its eagles.

Neither of them has unfortunately come down to us.

The 2nd Hussars: the NCOs

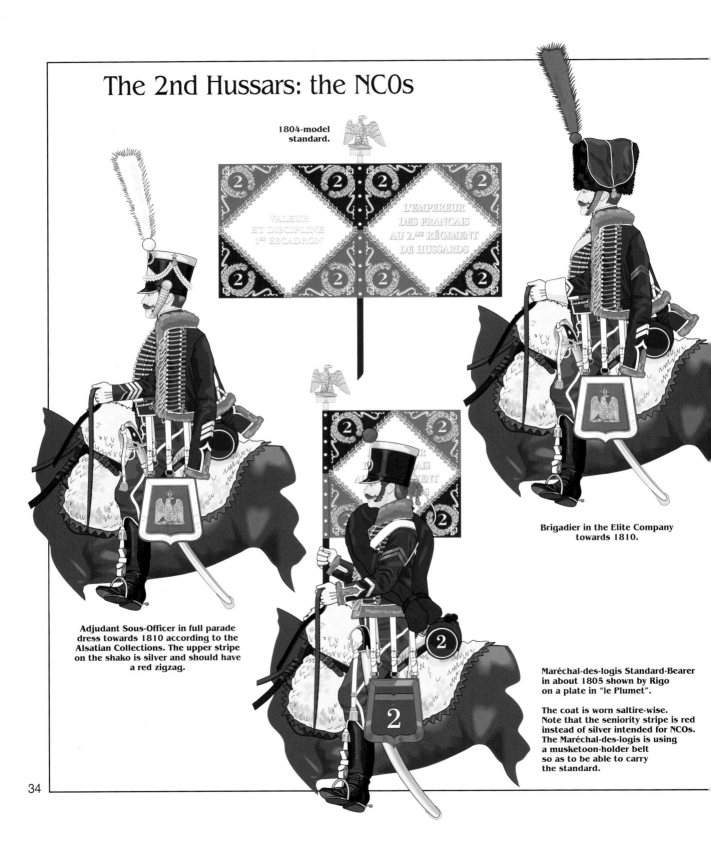

1804-model standard.

VALEUR ET DISCIPLINE 1ᴿ ESCADRON

L'EMPEREUR DES FRANCAIS AU 2.ᴹᴱ RÉGIMENT DE HUSSARDS

Adjudant Sous-Officer in full parade dress towards 1810 according to the Alsatian Collections. The upper stripe on the shako is silver and should have a red zigzag.

Brigadier in the Elite Company towards 1810.

Maréchal-des-logis Standard-Bearer in about 1805 shown by Rigo on a plate in "le Plumet".

The coat is worn saltire-wise. Note that the seniority stripe is red instead of silver intended for NCOs. The Maréchal-des-logis is using a musketoon-holder belt so as to be able to carry the standard.

The 2nd Hussars: the Trumpeters

Trumpeter in about 1805.
In the plate which inspired this illustration, Rigo supposed that Colonel Barbier had taken advantage of the fact that the Elite Company had been created to modify the uniform of at least some of the trumpeters in his regiment. Although the original drawing shows this trumpeter seen from the right-hand side, we have given him a sabretache. Indeed this item seems to have been indispensable to the Hussar's uniform and did not depend on whether or not the dolman or the pelisse was worn, as witnessed by the Hussar trumpeter uniform of the ancient Regime *(see Volume I).*

(see Volume I).

THE DOLMAN

This item showed the Hungarian origin of this corps and was an integral part of the prestige of the Hussars' uniform. The dolman was decorated on the torso with several braided rows of 18 buttons – sometimes 13 or 15.

The numbers of rows of buttons varied: the 1st, 3rd, 4th and 8th Regiments had five, whereas the others only had three; but these increased to five during the Empire.

Only the 2nd Hussars kept its original three rows longest. These progressive or immediate changes mean that there were a lot of variations within the same unit, meaning also several types of dolman decoration.

Trumpeter wearing full dress in about 1805.

Trumpeter wearing campaign dress in Spain around 1809.

The 2nd Hussars: the Trumpeters

Trumpeter belonging to the Elite Company in full dress in around 1810, according to the Carl Collection.

In the Alsatian Collections, the uniform is identical but with a red plume.

Trumpeter wearing full dress in about 1805 according to a drawing by L. Rousselot after a German engraving.

He is wearing the same dress as the troopers but with a different colour of plume. The shako, without a chinstrap, still has the cord attached across the trooper's chest.

Trumpeter towards 1810.

Note the strange red piping on the facings of the dolman.

The 2nd Hussars: the Officers

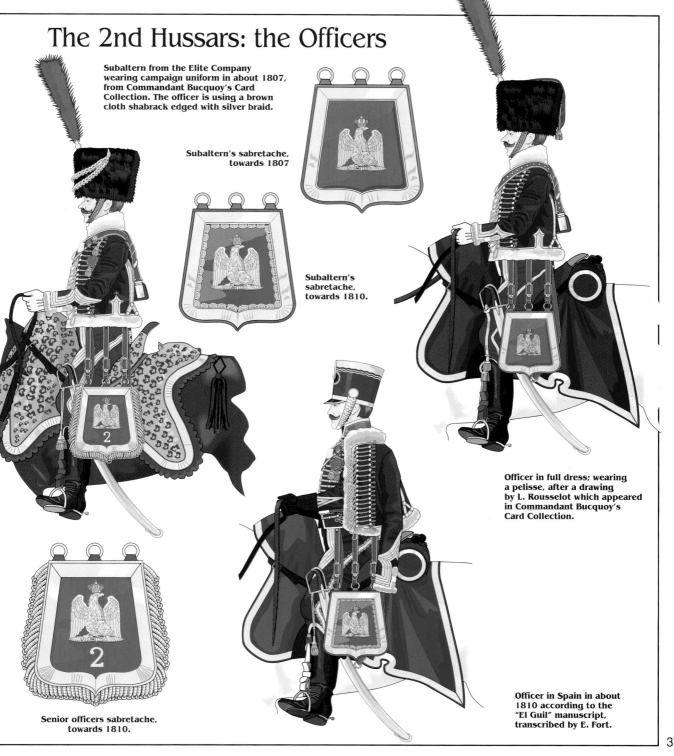

Subaltern from the Elite Company wearing campaign uniform in about 1807, from Commandant Bucquoy's Card Collection. The officer is using a brown cloth shabrack edged with silver braid.

Subaltern's sabretache, towards 1807

Subaltern's sabretache, towards 1810.

Officer in full dress; wearing a pelisse, after a drawing by L. Rousselot which appeared in Commandant Bucquoy's Card Collection.

Senior officers sabretache, towards 1810.

Officer in Spain in about 1810 according to the "El Guil" manuscript, transcribed by E. Fort.

37

The 3rd Hussar Regiment
(ex-Esterhazy)

Created under Louis XV as the *Esterhazy Regiment*, it was third in seniority in 1791.

The Argentine grey

It went through the first days of the Empire wearing the uniform of the Consulate which was argentine grey with red trimmings.

Although this may seem paradoxical, argentine grey did not correspond to its name. Many reproductions, closer to our time, give a shade of mouse grey with a touch of blue in the more or mess lighter shades.

When however we look more closely at the period reproductions this is no longer the case. There is one of an officer under the Ancien Regime preser-

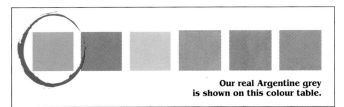

Our real Argentine grey is shown on this colour table.

ved in the museum at Nancy which gives argentine grey as much bluer. Martinet, the engraver who lived during the Empire, gives a greyer sky blue but with blue clearly dominating.

A miniature representing a Maréchal-des-Logis kept at the Musée de l'Armée gives a pale sky blue with a touch of grey. Continuing further, beyond the Empire, the description of the uniforms traced by Commandant Hecquet in 1828 shows argentine grey like the miniature in the Musée de l'Armée; the colour of the 3rd Hussars under the Second Empire carries on this tradition with a more intense shade.

There is no uniform item dating back to the 1st Empire to confirm that this colour was more sky blue than mouse grey.

However, without wishing to insist on anything without tangible proof, we have chosen to represent the Hussars from the 3rd Regiment wearing the colour surrounded above.

It is however possible that, because of the way colours were made at the time and because of the weather, the uniforms changed colour slightly and that there were several different shades of the same colour within the same unit.

In 1804, the Hussars of the 3rd Regiment still wore the cylindrical shako from the Consular period. They started to wear the flattened-cone shaped shako towards 1806-1807 when it bore a lozenge plate with a plaited cord, flounders and a black plume.

According to the studies carried out by Rigo, the braid and the loops were white in the Consular period, crimson towards 1805-1806, and then red again towards 1812 like they had been during the Ancien Regime. The NCOs used mixed blue and crimson plaited braid in about 1807.

Since the Revolution the straps were black. Some times because of supply problems, the equipment was made, at least partly, of white buffalo hide.

Trumpeters and the Regimental band

The trumpeters were dressed like the troopers but with the colours reversed. However, sometimes trumpeters are to be found wearing red and others crimson. Did these two colours co-exist or do they correspond to the change in the colour of the braid? It is impossible for us to confirm this.

It was during the Spanish Campaign that the regiment wore mourning for their Major-General Auguste de Colbert, killed in combat at Calcabellos on 3 January 1809.

The regiment did have a band of which traces exist in 1806 although we cannot be at all certain as to the number of musicians it had. Indeed its size depended on the amount of money the officer corps wanted to invest in such a unit.

At the time the regiment was under the command of Colonel Lebrun, who was none other than the son of the *"Arch-Treasurer"* of the Empire, and until recently the third Consul after Cambacérès and Bonaparte. It is possible that his fortune and his influence might have been used in the setting up and the presence of a band for his regiment.

The 3rd Hussars: the Troopers

Trooper wearing stable dress.

Sapper in full parade dress in about 1806 after a drawing by P. Benigni. Like the Sappers in the 1st Hussars, he must belong to the Elite Company. He is carrying a special sapper's axe modified for the cavalry (i.e. a smaller hatchet head mounted on a shorter shaft than on the infantry model).

Trooper from the Elite Company wearing campaign dress during the Polish Campaign (1807) according to a drawing by P. Benigni.

Trooper from the Elite Company in parade dress, about 1807.

39

The 3rd Hussars: the Troopers

Trooper's sabretache.

Note the civic crown over the number which indicates that this item can be identified as being the first type of sabretache described by Bertrand Malvaux.

Trooper in full parade dress in 1805.

P. Benigni has shown this trooper as being identical to the Consular period Hussar, wearing the cylindrical shako with the pennant rolled around the crown and with the visor most probably pinned on.

Trooper wearing campaign dress in 1806.

Trooper wearing full parade dress in 1808 according to A . Martinet.

The shako does not have a plate; the sabretache has a brass figure. The tips of the portmanteau are red, decorated with the figure 3 cut out of yellow cloth.

This trooper has been drawn by J. Girbal for one of Dr F.-G. Hourtoulle's plates showing Auguste de Colbert's brigade charging at the Battle of Jena.

The 3rd Hussars: the NCOs

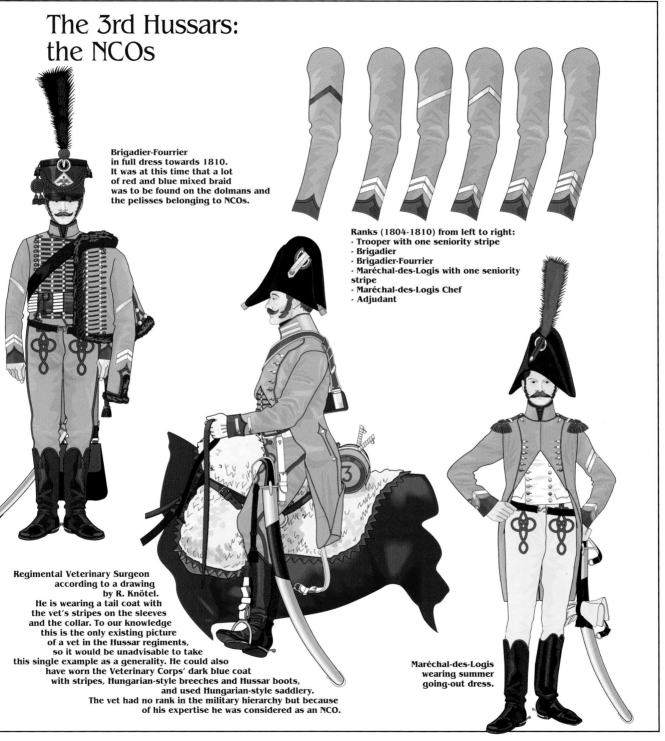

Brigadier-Fourrier
in full dress towards 1810.
It was at this time that a lot
of red and blue mixed braid
was to be found on the dolmans and
the pelisses belonging to NCOs.

Ranks (1804-1810) from left to right:
- **Trooper with one seniority stripe**
- **Brigadier**
- **Brigadier-Fourrier**
- **Maréchal-des-Logis with one seniority stripe**
- **Maréchal-des-Logis Chef**
- **Adjudant**

Regimental Veterinary Surgeon
according to a drawing
by R. Knötel.
He is wearing a tail coat with
the vet's stripes on the sleeves
and the collar. To our knowledge
this is the only existing picture
of a vet in the Hussar regiments,
so it would be unadvisable to take
this single example as a generality. He could also
have worn the Veterinary Corps' dark blue coat
with stripes, Hungarian-style breeches and Hussar boots,
and used Hungarian-style saddlery.
The vet had no rank in the military hierarchy but because
of his expertise he was considered as an NCO.

Maréchal-des-Logis
wearing summer
going-out dress.

The 3rd Hussars: the Trumpeters

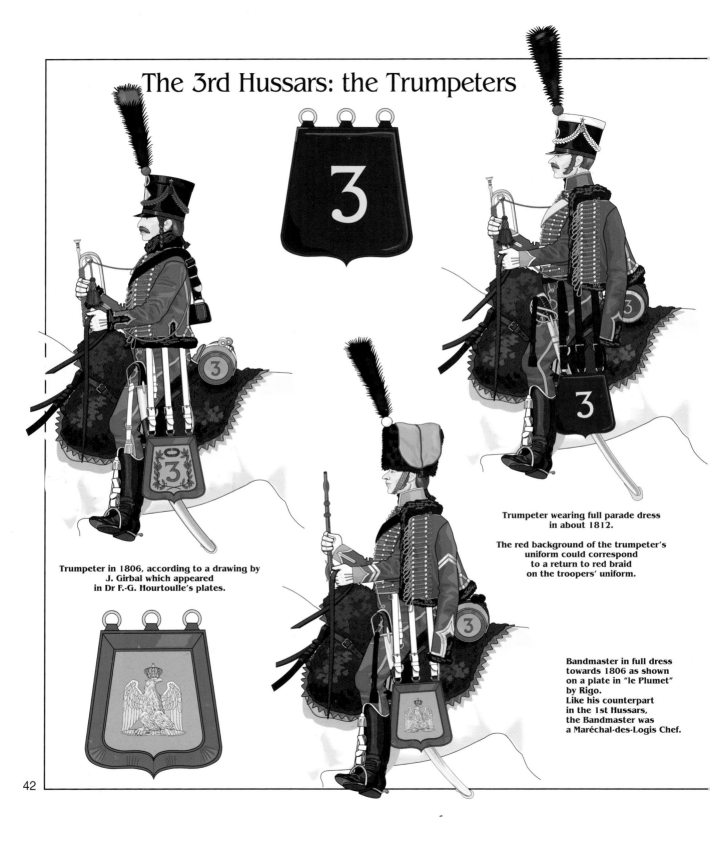

**Trumpeter in 1806, according to a drawing by
J. Girbal which appeared
in Dr F.-G. Hourtoulle's plates.**

**Trumpeter wearing full parade dress
in about 1812.**

**The red background of the trumpeter's
uniform could correspond
to a return to red braid
on the troopers' uniform.**

**Bandmaster in full dress
towards 1806 as shown
on a plate in "le Plumet"
by Rigo.
Like his counterpart
in the 1st Hussars,
the Bandmaster was
a Maréchal-des-Logis Chef.**

The 3rd Hussars: the Trumpeters

Trumpeter wearing campaign dress towards 1812, according to P. Benigni.

Trumpeter wearing full dress towards 1806, according to the Wurtz Collection.

Trumpeter from the Elite Company towards 1810, after a drawing by P.A. Leroux. Like the preceding horseman, this trumpeter's leatherwork is white, which was not customary in the regiment.

Trumpeter wearing campaign dress in about 1812. This is almost the same uniform, but the red has now been changed to crimson and the equipment leather is white.

43

The 3rd Hussars: the Officers

Officer wearing campaign dress
in about 1806, after a drawing by J. Girbal
in the set of plates for Dr F.-G. Hourtoulle.

Senior Officer wearing full parade dress
in 1809, after a drawing by P. Benigni.

The white plume indicates that this officer
was on the regimental headquarters staff.

Subaltern in about 1806,
according to a drawing
by L. Rousselot.

44

The 3rd Hussars: the Officers

Major wearing full parade dress
after a drawing by H. Knötel.

The shabrack is edged with gold
and silver braid denoting
the horseman's rank (Major).
The sabretache belonging
to senior officers was often edged
with cabled fringes.

Senior Officer after the set
of drawings by A. Martinet.

The 4th Hussar Regiment
(ex-Colonel-général)

The regiment was created in 1793 for the Duc de Chartres (who later became the Duc d'Orléans, then *Philippe-Egalité*) who was appointed the *Colonel-General* of the Hussars five years earlier. It was fifth in seniority, then fourth when the 4th – the former Saxon Hussars – emigrated.

The regiment kept the colours it had when it was created. The yellow braid border around the dolman's plaits which was the Colonel-General regiment's distinctive, was suppressed under the Republic.

Uniforms

The shakoes did not appear before the 1806-1807 directives. They were decorated with a cockade held in place by yellow braid as shown in the Zimmermann Manuscript, even though the proportions of the shako do seem rather strange. In about 1808-1809, a lozenge-shaped plate stamped with an eagle and the regimental number was added and the tie cord was replaced by scale chinstraps.

From the beginning of the Empire the dolman had three rows of buttons which were quickly changed to five. The collar was dark blue. The Zimmermann Manuscript however gives it as being red which according to L. Rousselot, is a mistake.

The pelisse was scarlet and no major modifications were made to it; it only got shorter, like the dolman, as was the fashion during the Empire.

At the beginning of the Empire, the top of the sabretache flap had an embroidered cloth background and was held in place by a stripe the same colour as the braid. When used on campaign this costly item was protected from bad weather by a leather cover with the regimental number painted on it, or with a brass number.

The war squadrons were in Spain from 1809 onwards. On Plate 82, L. Rousselot thinks that because of the problems of obtaining supplies from France, certain items – in particular riding breeches – were tailored from local brown cloth. The part of the regiment which remained in Germany was reviewed by General Bourcier the same year. It seems that the detachment did not have any pelisses or Hungarian breeches, but only dolmans and canvas trousers.

Once again this shows that the modern picture we have of the Hussar wearing a complete uniform as though he were on parade is very far from the reality of the period.

Trumpeters

The trumpeters wore the same colours as the troopers but reversed. Towards 1808, the red felt shako was decorated with the troopers' cords and plumes. The Hungarian breeches were scarlet although some sources do show them as being dark blue. Some of the changes in uniform were also caused by the extravagance and wishes of successive regimental Colonels.

A Spanish document taken up by L. Rousselot shows a Trumpet-Major wearing braid on the pelisse and on the dolman which is a mix of gold and scarlet like that on the upper stripe of the shako.

During the whole of the Empire, the officers wore the same uniform as the troopers but with gold trimmings.

The systematic approach in the engravings by A Martinet shows us a uniform which was identical to that of the other regiments, with only the distinctive colours changing. The panther-skin shabrack was normally for the wealthier subalterns. The other officers had to make do with a cloth shabrack edged with a gold thread stripe.

As the 4th Hussars had taken part at the Battle of Austerlitz, they were awarded two gold crowns for their eagles by the City of Paris.

It was only on 27 September 1808, when the regiment returned to France on its way to Spain that it received these two crowns which decorated their Model-1804 standards. Only the standard belonging to the 1st Squadron, preserved at the Musée de l'Armée, has come down to us; unfortunately it had not been decorated with a crown.

The 4th Hussars: the Troopers

Trooper in about 1806-1807 after the set of Zimmermann plates.

The little cord at the rear of the shako does not seem to have any real use. Indeed in normal times it went around the neck and across the horseman's chest. Moreover, the shako seems to be shorter than usual. On the dolman, a shoulder flap – which in itself is unusual – supports the equipment.

Trooper from the Elite Company, in about 1812, according to a drawing by L. Rousselot.

Trooper from an ordinary company, about 1810.

Trooper from the Elite Company in around 1812, after a plate in "le Plumet".

Trooper from the Elite Company towards 1805 according to a gouache by Colonel Barbier.

The 4th Hussars: the Troopers

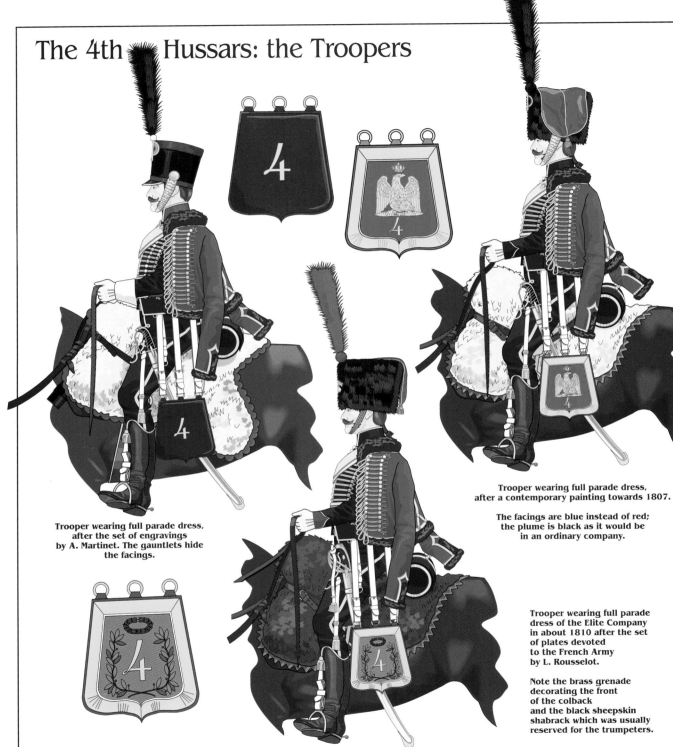

Trooper wearing full parade dress,
after the set of engravings
by A. Martinet. The gauntlets hide
the facings.

Trooper wearing full parade dress,
after a contemporary painting towards 1807.

The facings are blue instead of red;
the plume is black as it would be
in an ordinary company.

Trooper wearing full parade
dress of the Elite Company
in about 1810 after the set
of plates devoted
to the French Army
by L. Rousselot.

Note the brass grenade
decorating the front
of the colback
and the black sheepskin
shabrack which was usually
reserved for the trumpeters.

The 4th Hussars: the Trumpeters

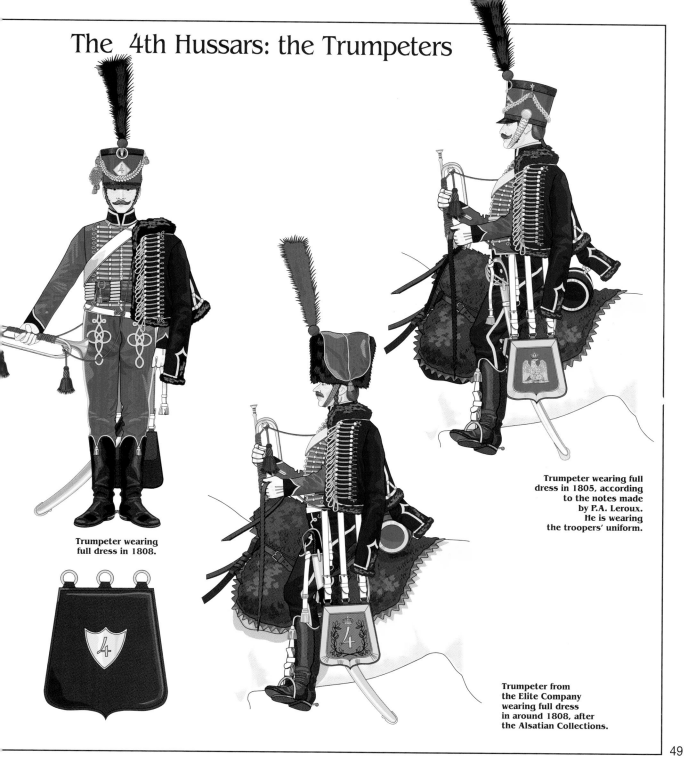

Trumpeter wearing
full dress in 1808.

Trumpeter wearing full
dress in 1805, according
to the notes made
by P.A. Leroux.
He is wearing
the troopers' uniform.

Trumpeter from
the Elite Company
wearing full dress
in around 1808, after
the Alsatian Collections.

The 4th Hussars: the Trumpeters

Trumpeter wearing campaign dress, according to a painting by E. Detaille and taken up in the plates by L. Rousselot devoted to the 4th Hussars.

Trumpeter in full parade dress in 1809.

Maréchal-des-Logis Trompette-Major wearing marching dress in about 1810 during the Spanish Campaign. This uniform was published by L. Rousselot in his plate on the 4th Hussars. Note the shoulder flap ending in a trefoil.

Bandmaster appearing in an edition of "Passepoil" according to a drawing by E. Leliepvre taken from the Alsatian Collections.

The 5th Hussars: the NCOs

Obverse of o the 1804-type
standard of the regiment.

**L'EMPEREUR
DES FRANÇAIS
AU 5.ME RÉGIMENT
DE HUSSARDS**

Maréchal-des-Logis in about
1807 after the card collection
belonging to Commandant
Bucquoy.

Adjudant wearing full parade
dress towards 1805.

He is carrying the stick corresponding
to his function. This tradition came from
the Prussian and Austrian cavalries.
It is important not to forget that
the Hussars were of Hungarian origin
and that recruitment during
the Ancien Regime was mainly among
the Germans.

Maréchal-des-Logis
Standard-Bearer
about 1807 after a drawing
by L. Rousselot.

Standards

The regiment had four 1804-
model standards each carried
by an NCO.

Captured in Paris in 1815 by
the Allies, they disappeared
during World War Two.

The 5th Hussars: the Trumpeters

Town coat belonging to a trumpeter in about 1807-1808.

This dates from the first half of the Empire because the turnbacks on the coat are hooked up. From 1810 onwards, the tails of the coat were shorter and the turnbacks were sown onto the skirts.

Trumpeter wearing parade dress towards 1810 according to H. Knötel.

Trumpeter wearing town dress in about 1807-1808. This uniform was drawn by Rigo on a plate in "le Plumet".

Trumpeter wearing parade dress, 1808-1809.

On this plate, Rigo gives us this uniform which is almost identical to the one shown above, except for the facings, the sabretache flap and the trumpet cord. As for the completely blue shako, there are two possibilities here: either it is a headdress made of felt then dyed blue; or it is a standard model but to which a blue stripe has been added to the folded part of the crown.

56

The 5th Hussars: the Trumpeters

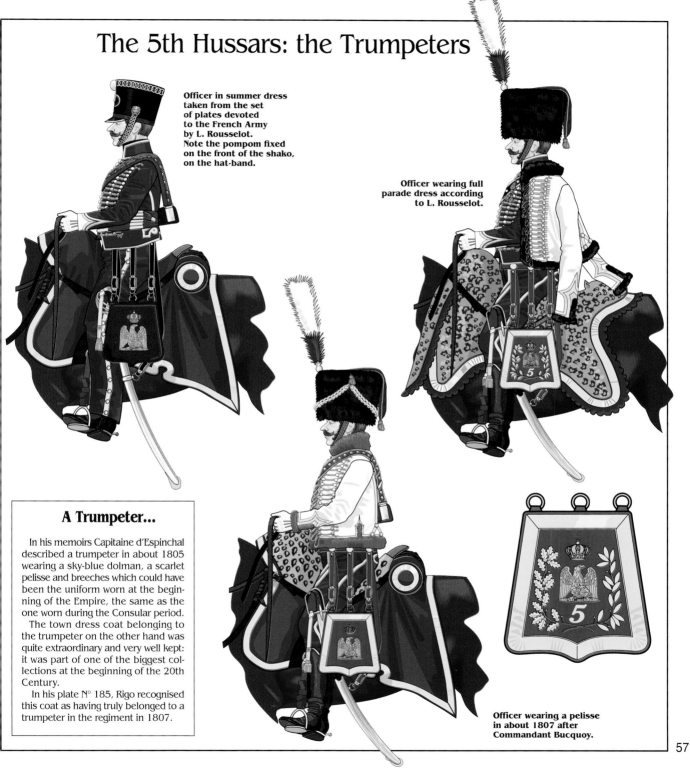

Officer in summer dress
taken from the set
of plates devoted
to the French Army
by L. Rousselot.
Note the pompom fixed
on the front of the shako,
on the hat-band.

Officer wearing full
parade dress according
to L. Rousselot.

A Trumpeter...

In his memoirs Capitaine d'Espinchal
described a trumpeter in about 1805
wearing a sky-blue dolman, a scarlet
pelisse and breeches which could have
been the uniform worn at the beginning of the Empire, the same as the
one worn during the Consular period.

The town dress coat belonging to
the trumpeter on the other hand was
quite extraordinary and very well kept:
it was part of one of the biggest collections at the beginning of the 20th
Century.

In his plate N° 185, Rigo recognised
this coat as having truly belonged to a
trumpeter in the regiment in 1807.

Officer wearing a pelisse
in about 1807 after
Commandant Bucquoy.

The 5th Hussars: the Officers

The Squadrons in 1810

In 1810, after a sixth squadron was created, the regiment was thus constituted. It is obvious that no regiment was ever able to get up to full strength, even before the departure for Russia.

- **1st squadron**
  1st company or Elite company
  7th company
- **2nd squadron**
  2nd company
  8th company
- **3rd squadron**
  3rd company
  9th company

- **4th squadron**
  4th company
  10th company
- **5th squadron**
  5th company
  11th company
- **6th squadron**
  6th company
  12th company

Details of flounders belonging to the shako of an officer in the 5th Hussars

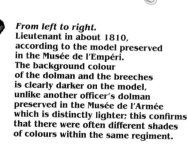

Senior Officer wearing full parade dress after H. Knötel.

From left to right.
Lieutenant in about 1810, according to the model preserved in the Musée de l'Empéri. The background colour of the dolman and the breeches is clearly darker on the model, unlike another officer's dolman preserved in the Musée de l'Armée which is distinctly lighter; this confirms that there were often different shades of colours within the same regiment.

Lieutenant in about 1807, after a contemporary German engraving.

Officer in social dress towards 1810.

The 5th Hussars: the Colonels

Uniform worn by Colonel Meuziau in about 1810

This illustration of the Colonel who was the subject of a plate by Rigo in "le Plumet" was taken from a contemporary portrait. He is already wearing ample riding breeches with false boots at the bottom made of black leather which proves that General Lasalle was not the only one to wear this rarely-worn item of clothing.

Colonel wearing gala dress in about 1806.

He is wearing a plume made of heron feathers, the distinctive sign of the regimental commanding officer and a double upper stripe on the shako.

Uniform worn by Colonel Schwarz in 1806. This was drawn by J. Girbal for one of Dr F.-G. Hourtoulle's plates. The illustration was inspired by a naïve contemporary portrait.

The 6th Hussar Regiment

On 2 September 1792, Citizen Boyer, a former *"Taker of the Bastille"*, was authorised to levy a corps of volunteers called the *"Defenders of liberty and equality Hussars"*; shortly afterwards they were incorporated into the Hussar Corps as the 7th Regiment, then the 6th In June 1793.

In 1805, the 6th Hussars was the first regiment to adopt the lozenge-shaped plate with an eagle and the number of the regiment stamped on it. In about 1807, a plaited cord and scale chinstrap were added. In 1808, the shako became entirely red until it was replaced just before the Russian Campaign by a cylindrical shako of the same colour. It seems that here again, the 6th Regiment was the first to adopt this new hat, the shako rouleau – cylindrical shako. The pompom – whose colour indicated to which company the rider belonged – was attached to the shako by means of a little metal strip inserted through a loop.

At the beginning of the Empire, the dolman had three rows of buttons but this was quickly increased to five. The collar which had been scarlet during the Consulate was blue during the Empire. The seniority stripes were usually red but as the colour of the dolman hid them, for the troopers they were the same colour as the braid.

The sabretache did not change between 1805 and 1812 although here we do show different examples of embroidery; however, there were no sabretaches made entirely of leather before the end of the Empire.

Officer and NCOs

The NCO which R. Forthoffer noted down, after Gunner *Hahlo's manuscript*, was wearing a tawny skin colback which was not often encountered on this type of headdress. The sabretache was covered with a sheath whose top was made of fur the same tawny colour as the colback. The trumpeter wore the uniform with the colours reversed. A completely red uniform appeared in about 1808-1809. The officers were dressed like the rest of the troopers but the yellow was replaced by gold.

There are very few documents showing officers of the 6th Hussars during the Empire except for Martinet's engravings which show the distinctive colours but whose principle of systematic drawing does not reveal certain regimental particularities.

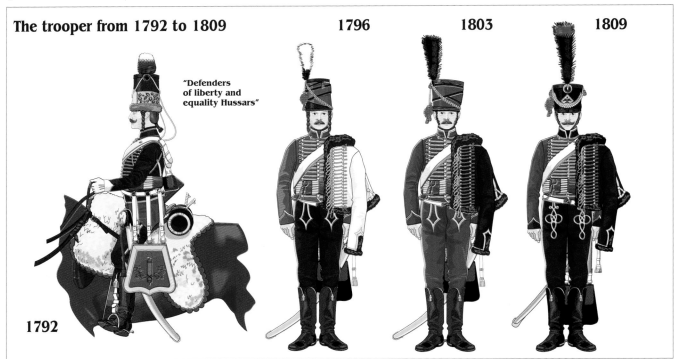

The trooper from 1792 to 1809   1796   1803   1809

"Defenders of liberty and equality Hussars"

1792

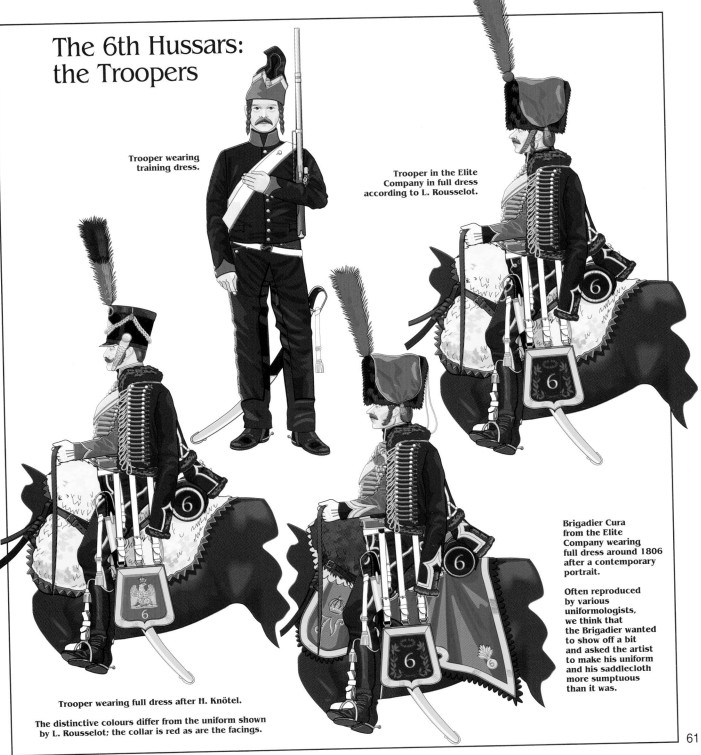

The 6th Hussars: the Troopers

Trooper wearing training dress.

Trooper in the Elite Company in full dress according to L. Rousselot.

Trooper wearing full dress after H. Knötel.

The distinctive colours differ from the uniform shown by L. Rousselot; the collar is red as are the facings.

Brigadier Cura from the Elite Company wearing full dress around 1806 after a contemporary portrait.

Often reproduced by various uniformologists, we think that the Brigadier wanted to show off a bit and asked the artist to make his uniform and his saddlecloth more sumptuous than it was.

The 6th Hussars: the Trumpeters

Trumpeter from an ordinary company wearing full parade dress around 1809 according to a study which appeared in a bulletin of "le Briquet".

Trumpeter from the Elite Company wearing full parade dress about 1809 according to a study which appeared in a bulletin of "le Briquet".

The Elite Company

The Elite Company's uniform is known thanks to a naïve contemporary portrait.

The Brigadier who had his portrait made certainly wanted to show off and asked the artist to show him in a brilliant uniform.

Indeed it seems unlikely that the Elite Company was fitted out with a scalloped braid saddlecloth with an embroidered "N", but rather like the rest of the troopers, with the usual sheepskin shabrack.

Trumpeter from the Elite Company wearing full parade dress around 1809.

The 6th Hussars: the Trumpeters

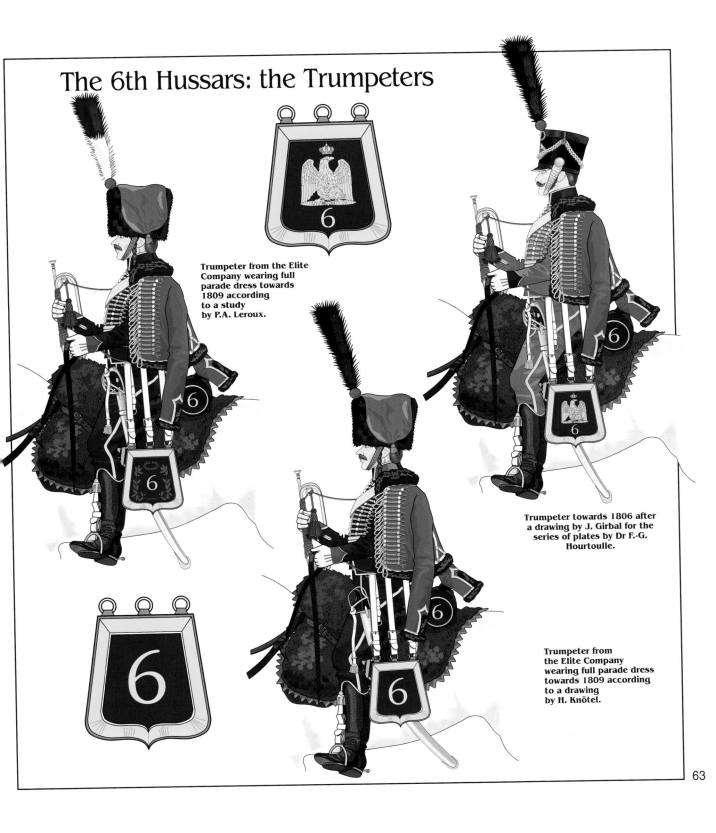

Trumpeter from the Elite
Company wearing full
parade dress towards
1809 according
to a study
by P.A. Leroux.

Trumpeter towards 1806 after
a drawing by J. Girbal for the
series of plates by Dr F.-G.
Hourtoulle.

Trumpeter from
the Elite Company
wearing full parade dress
towards 1809 according
to a drawing
by H. Knötel.

The 6th Hussars: the Officers and the NCOs

6th Hussar Regiment Standards

Like all the Hussar regiments the 6th received four 1804-model Eagles.

Maréchal-des-Logis Chef in Spain towards 1809.

Made from a manuscript by Gunner Hahlo, assigned to the Westphalian Artillery in Spain. The sabretache which is not shown from the front here has been covered with a tawny fur-covered sheath, the same as that of the fur of the pelisse. This document was entirely taken up by R. Forthoffer and completed from historical and uniform commentaries.

Senior Officer towards 1810 according to an aquarelle by H. Knötel.

General Pajol and the 6th Hussar Regiment

On a plate for Dr F.-G. Hourtoulle, J. Girbal shows Pajol, at the time a Colonel with the 6th Hussars in 1805.

This fiery horseman is wearing a shako with neither visor nor plate, decorated with a string of gold braid rings on the upper part and surmounted by a white aigrette. He is accompanied by Brigadier Joseph Cura, from the Elite Company whose uniform and saddlery recall those of the Brigadier on page 61.

The 7th Hussar Regiment

On 23 November 1792, *Lamothe's Hussars*, a unit of volunteer Hussars of the Revolution, were incorporated into the Hussar arm with Kellermann's Legion, the remnants of the *Saxe Hussars* and a *Royal Allemand* squadron which remained loyal to the Republic. At first eighth in rank in the arm, they became 7th when the Saxon Hussars were written off the rolls.

In 1804, the regiment already had a shako without a plate. With the dispositions of 1806, it was given a lozenge-shaped plate stamped with an eagle and the number of the regiment as well as scale chinstraps. In around 1808, the black plume was replaced by a white one with a red tip then in 1810, it was half green and half red, and the lozenge plate was replaced by a cut out eagle mounted on a base.

The Musée de l'Empéri shows a trooper with a red shako and a yellow hat-band which we cannot confirm because L. Rousselot has shown these cavalrymen with a black shako during the Russian Campaign.

The dolman was dark green with three rows of buttons then five towards 1807.

L. Rousselot shows us a rather fancy uniform for a Maréchal-des-logis from the Elite Company enriched with trimmings on the dolman and the pelisse, showing very well how important it was to be elegant when one was a Hussar.

An inspection made by General Laurent on 27 July 1805 revealed again what was missing in the Hussars' uniform. He notes:

"The two Adjudant NCOs are armed with a pair of pistols and a sabre like the NCOs. The 11 regimental pupils and the workmen only have sabres. The brigadiers and the troopers only have a pair of pistols each, a musketoon and a sabre.

Now the armament was far from being complete and out of all the musketoons, half were foreign-built and without bayonets."

The general complained that the forage caps did not correspond to the ordnances, that the regiment did not have any overcoats and that the Hussars had replaced them with short jackets.

With this report, it is interesting to note the presence of regimental pupils, whose uniform is unknown, and master workmen for whom H. Malibran describes a dark green tail coat in about 1812. These master craftsmen were organised by their crafts: saddler, armourer, and tailor.

Unfortunately history has not recorded what these obscure men wore for uniforms, even though they were indispensable for the regiment's well-being.

The officers were dressed in the colours of the regiment with gold buttons and trimmings. A drawing by H. Knötel shows an officer wearing green Hungarian breeches which is a little strange, unless it was a second uniform. This does not seem likely however since the 7th Hussars had worn red ever since they were created or almost.

The regiment was given four 1804-model standards. P. Charrié wrote in his book about the First Empire's standards and flags that a single standard was kept in a private collection without mentioning when and what happened to it afterwards.

The HUSSAR REGIMENT in 1812

The Hussar Regiments towards 1812 comprised two-company squadrons and a headquarters. The regiment was formed by 6 Squadrons.

Headquarters
— 1 Colonel
— 1 Major
— 2 Squadron commanders
— 1 Quarter-master-Pay-master
— 1 Surgeon-major
— 1 Surgeon *aide-major*
— 1 Mail Orderly
— 2 Surgeons *sous-aides-majors*
— 2 Veterinary officers
— 2 adjudants NCOs

— 1 Trumpet-brigadier
— 4 Masters craftsmen
   1 Armourer
   1 Saddler
   1 Tailor
   1 Cobbler
— and few pupils

The Company
— 1 Captain
— 1 Lieutenant
— 2 Second-lieutenants
— 1 *Maréchal-des-logis chef*
— 4 *Maréchaux-des-logis*
— 1 *Brigadier-fourrier*
— 8 *Brigadiers*
— 2 trumpeters
— 1 Blacksmith
— 108 Hussars

The 7th Hussars: the Troopers

Trooper in full parade dress towards 1807.
Period engraving by Basset conserved at *the Musée de l'Empéri*. The little plume gives a rather original note to the Hussar's uniform. When the background of the sabretache is green it is a paler shade than that of the uniform.

Trooper wearing full parade dress towards 1811 according to an engraving by A. Martinet. The white plume with red tip replaced the one used previously, and the sabretache is now red instead of green.

Trooper wearing campaign dress around 1806-1808.

The 7th Hussars: the Troopers

Town dress towards 1806 drawn by the "Burger of Hamburg".

Campaign dress. Note the regulation scarlet waistcoat showing through the opening of the pelisse.

Trooper in the Elite Company according to a plate by L. Rousselot. The sabre loops seem to be made of natural leather.

Summer dress according to a model in the Musée de l'Armée.

RIDING TROUSERS

"His Majesty the Emperor has ordered that cloth trousers with sheepskin are to be added to the articles making up the uniform of the Hussar arm as of 1 January 1810; they should last two years."

(Imperial Decree of 7 July 1809.)

The Emperor thus regulated the almost permanent use of the stable trousers which replaced the cloth breeches more and more often on different occasions. As can be noticed, the description of this particular article still remains rather "wooly".

This very short Imperial description partly explains why there were so many differences between the charivari of the Hussar regiments during this period.

The trousers were green with a stripe the same colour as the Hungarian breeches.

The 7th Hussars: the Troopers

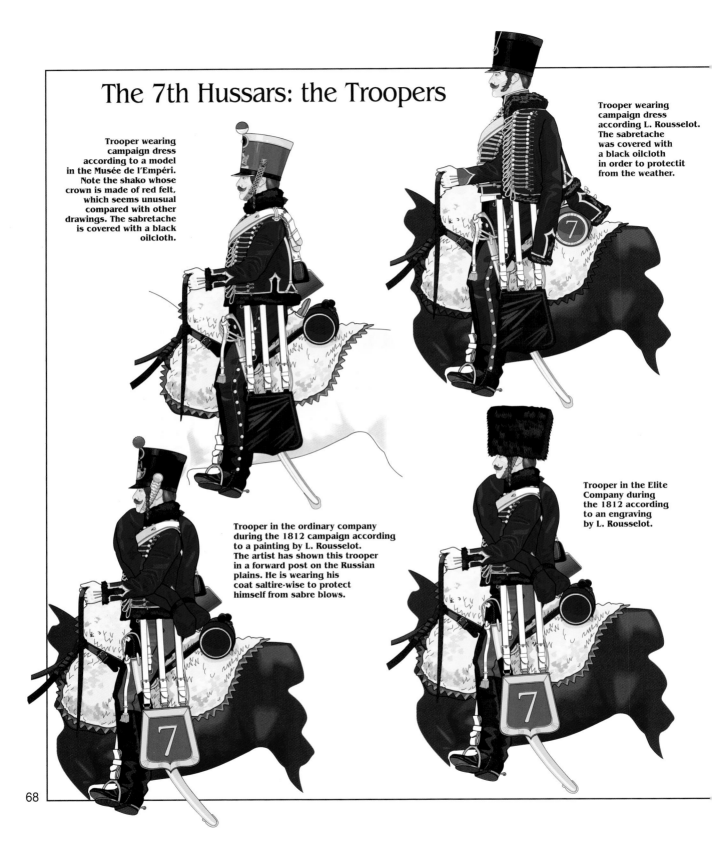

Trooper wearing campaign dress according to a model in the Musée de l'Empéri. Note the shako whose crown is made of red felt, which seems unusual compared with other drawings. The sabretache is covered with a black oilcloth.

Trooper wearing campaign dress according L. Rousselot. The sabretache was covered with a black oilcloth in order to protectit from the weather.

Trooper in the ordinary company during the 1812 campaign according to a painting by L. Rousselot. The artist has shown this trooper in a forward post on the Russian plains. He is wearing his coat saltire-wise to protect himself from sabre blows.

Trooper in the Elite Company during the 1812 according to an engraving by L. Rousselot.

The 7th Hussars: the NCOs

Brigadier-Fourrier wearing campaign dress.

The uniform has been recreated by a reconstitution group who wants to get the uniforms of the 7th Hussars to live again.

Adjudant Sous-Officier towards 1810 according to a drawing by R. Louis.

Note that the artist has respected the zigzag of the upper stripe on the adjudant's shako.

An NCO's extravagant uniform according to a drawing by L. Rousselot.

Brigadier in training uniform.

The 7th Hussars: the Trumpeters

Trumpeter wearing town dress in about 1807-1808.

This trumpeter from the Elite Company wearing full parade dress in about 1809, was the subject of a plate by Rigo.

Trumpeter wearing full parade dress towards 1811 according to P.A. Leroux. Note that the sabretache is the same model as the troopers'.

Trumpeter from the Elite Company wearing full parade dress towards 1809.

Although the colours of the trumpeter were reversed compared to those of the troopers, the green was a paler shade of green.

The 7th Hussars: the Trumpeters

Trumpeter from the Elite Company in about 1806 according to a drawing by J. Girbal for Dr F.-G. Hourtoulle's plates.

The colback made of tawny fur is unusual in that it was traditionally made of black, or white for the trumpeters, bearskin.

Trumpeter from the Elite Company towards 1811 after a drawing by Richard Knötel in the set of plates in his "UniformKunde"

The Trumpeters

The trumpeter's uniform has the colours reversed with a lighter shade of green like the troopers'.

The shako was light green edged with black with the troopers'plume; it evolved in the same manner. R. Knötel gives us a trumpeter from the Elite Company entirely in red with a white shabrack which is an ensemble whose colours are hardly usual for the regiment.

A drawing by P.A. Leroux shows white braid and loops for a trumpeter which does not seem very likely either especially for a regiment whose distinctive was yellow.

Trumpeter towards 1808 according to P.A. leroux.

71

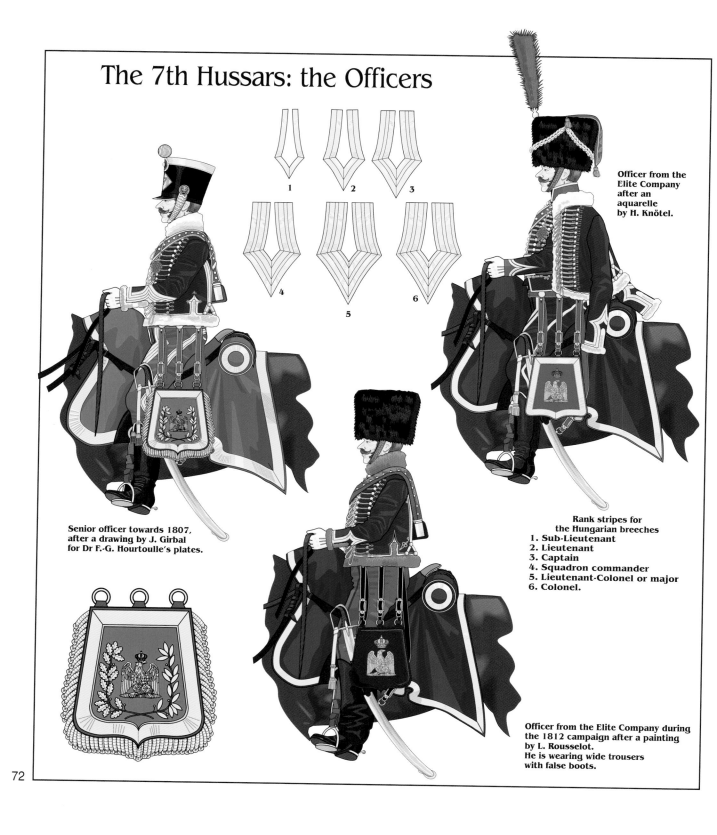

The 7th Hussars: the Officers

Officer from the Elite Company after an aquarelle by H. Knötel.

Senior officer towards 1807, after a drawing by J. Girbal for Dr F.-G. Hourtoulle's plates.

Rank stripes for the Hungarian breeches
1. Sub-Lieutenant
2. Lieutenant
3. Captain
4. Squadron commander
5. Lieutenant-Colonel or major
6. Colonel.

Officer from the Elite Company during the 1812 campaign after a painting by L. Rousselot.
He is wearing wide trousers with false boots.

The 8th Hussar Regiment

The 8th Hussars were related to the former *Fabre-fons Hussars* created during the Revolution.

There is no plate on the shako but it does have a cockade in the upper part of the headdress, held in place by white braid.

A cord keeps the shako on the horseman's head. In about 1807, white metal scale chinstraps were added. In 1809, the white plaited cord was replaced by a red and green one.

A short time afterwards, the crown of the shako became red and the centrally-positioned cockade was held in place by dark green braid.

Uniform

At the beginning of the Empire, the dolman had five rows of buttons with white braid and plaits. In 1808, the trimmings were a mix of 2/3 red and 1/3 green. Some contemporary drawings show troopers with entirely red braid or red and black braid. It could be that this type of trimming existed alongside the others at the same time, just as it could also be a mistake in the reproduction of the pictures, because the techniques of the time did not allow this type of detail to be reproduced very clearly. In 1804, the breeches had white side seem stripes and the Hungarian knots were white; they were changed to green when the new colours adopted for the trimmings changed to red and green.

The red breeches worn mainly during the Empire existed alongside the green breeches already in use during the Consulate. It is possible that these breeches were kept for use as a second uniform or town dress.

In about 1812, the Hussars used riding breeches with black sheepskin on the inside with false leather boots sewn into the bottom of the trousers. This item has already been noted with the 7th Hussars during the same period.

In around 1809, the Elite Company wore a colback with a copper grenade decorating the front; this has already been seen with their counterparts in the 4th Hussars.

The sabretache had an embroidered white eagle and was edged with a black stripe; it was used until 1812 when it was replaced by a leather model with the number cut out of white metal. P. Benigni made a drawing showing barrack dress for Adjudant NCOs. They are wearing an overcoat with one epaulette instead of the normal two for their rank, which was current practise in the Light Cavalry but not a general rule, and the troopers' breeches without the stripe of rank.

The officers

The officers wore the same uniform as the troopers with silver trimmings.

The officers at the end of the Consular period are known particularly well thanks to the set of portraits made by Boos and offered by the same officers to Colonel Marulaz, in command of the regiment at the time. Some of these portraits are displayed in the *Musée de l'Armée* which shows us that the green colour of the pelisse has tended to turn to sky blue with age. In the same museum the complete uniform belonging to a Squadron Commander of around 1812 can be seen; it is in perfect condition. The pelisse and the dolman are quite clearly shorter than in 1804 and the shako also respects the fashion of the times with its string of silver embroidered rings on the upper part and a chinstrap with a small chain attached to two lion muzzles. The regiment was given two 1804-model standards. Only one has survived, that belonging to the 4th Squadron, kept in Berlin; but it was sold in 1911 and all trace of it has been lost.

Squadron Commander in around 1812.
This is a model showing an entire 8th Hussars officer's uniform. Note that the pelisse and the dolman have become shorter since the beginning of the Empire. The shako is decorated with a string of silver-thread embroidered "zigzags" along the top part and the chinstrap is made up of a small chain mounted on a leather thong. The officer is armed with an oriental-style sword.

The 8th hussars: the Troopers

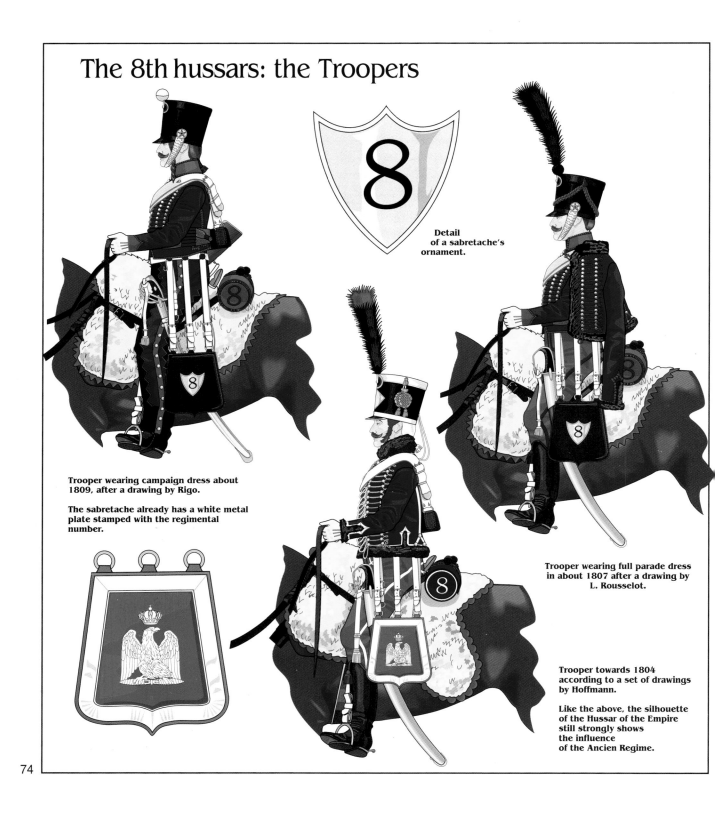

Detail
of a sabretache's
ornament.

Trooper wearing campaign dress about
1809, after a drawing by Rigo.

The sabretache already has a white metal
plate stamped with the regimental
number.

Trooper wearing full parade dress
in about 1807 after a drawing by
L. Rousselot.

Trooper towards 1804
according to a set of drawings
by Hoffmann.

Like the above, the silhouette
of the Hussar of the Empire
still strongly shows
the influence
of the Ancien Regime.

74

The 8th hussars: the Troopers

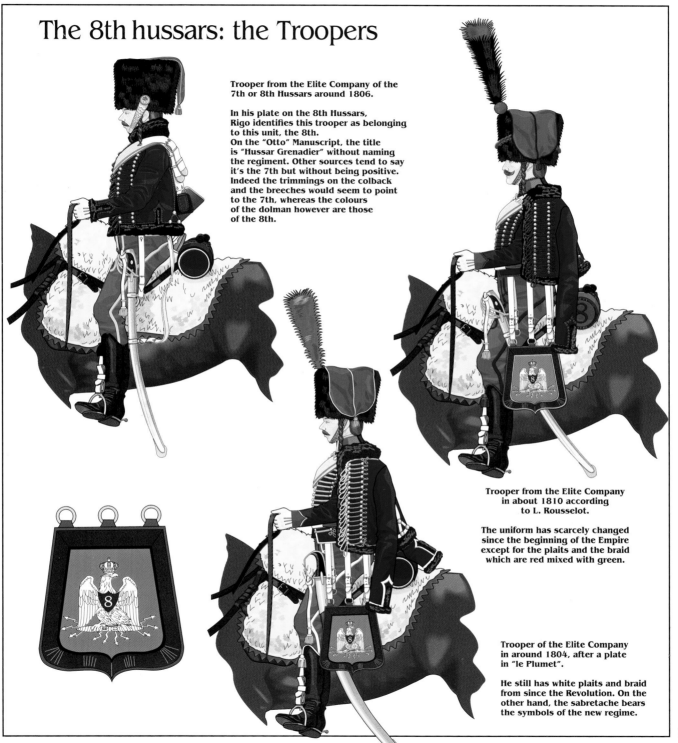

Trooper from the Elite Company of the 7th or 8th Hussars around 1806.

In his plate on the 8th Hussars, Rigo identifies this trooper as belonging to this unit, the 8th.
On the "Otto" Manuscript, the title is "Hussar Grenadier" without naming the regiment. Other sources tend to say it's the 7th but without being positive. Indeed the trimmings on the colback and the breeches would seem to point to the 7th, whereas the colours of the dolman however are those of the 8th.

Trooper from the Elite Company in about 1810 according to L. Rousselot.

The uniform has scarcely changed since the beginning of the Empire except for the plaits and the braid which are red mixed with green.

Trooper of the Elite Company in around 1804, after a plate in "le Plumet".

He still has white plaits and braid from since the Revolution. On the other hand, the sabretache bears the symbols of the new regime.

The 8th hussars: the Troopers

Trooper wearing town dress in around 1808, after a German engraving.

Trooper from an ordinary company in full dress, after an aquarelle by H. Knötel.

Trooper from the Elite Company in campaign dress, in around 1812.

Apart from the inside sheepskins, the riding breeches have leather false boots sewn into the bottom of the trousers.

8

Trooper wearing full dress in around 1812, according to a contemporary drawing by Albrecht Adam.

The 8th hussars: the Troopers and the NCOs

Adjudant's Forage cap.

Trooper from the Elite Company around 1810 in campaign dress, according to a drawing by L. Rousselot.

Trooper in training uniform.

Rank epaulette for an Adjudant.

Adjudant, after a German engraving by Geissler in about 1808.

This week-day uniform could be the same as the social dress or summer going-out dress. The NCO is wearing an overcoat with only one rank epaulette, on the left, as was often the case in the Light Cavalry.

Adjudant wearing barracks dress, after a German engraving by Geissler towards 1808.

The 8th hussars: the Trumpeters

The Trumpeters

A town dress uniform drawn by P. Benigni in 1804 shows a trumpeter wearing an entirely red uniform with white trimmings. It is possible that the full dress with sabre and sabretache was identical. During this same period, the colours of the trumpeters' uniforms were the reverse of those of the regiment, with green plaits on the pelisse and the dolman, and red stripes on the green breeches.

Likewise, A. Adam recorded a trumpeter from an ordinary company with red and green plaits.

Trumpeter in service dress in around 1811, according to the set of drawings by R. Knötel which appeared in "Uniformenkunde". We have given him an embroidered sabretache which remained in use until 1812.

Trumpeter in town dress in around 1807, after a German engraving by Geissler.

Note that the shape of the colback is rather cylindrical and that the belt and the sabre-knot are black.

Trumpeter wearing full parade dress, towards 1807.

78

The 8th hussars: the Trumpeters

Detail
of a trumpeter's
sabretache.
from the Elite
Company.

Trumpeter wearing campaign dress in 1812,
according to a contemporary drawing by
Albrecht Adam.

The riding breeches incorporate the leather
false boots sewn into the bottom of the
trousers.

Detail of the colback's grenade.

Trumpeter from the Elite Company
wearing full parade dress in about 1810,
mounted and on foot.

This trumpeter comes from the collection
of cards by Commandant Bucquoy and on
his colback there is a brass grenade with
the number 8 on it. Although this
decoration is rather rarely attested, it
does also appear in the Elite Company of
the 4th Hussars.

The 8th hussars: the Officers

Captain in the Elite Company around 1809, after R. Knötel.

It seems that the pelisse edged with white was used by the officers of the 8th Hussars, at least at the beginning of the Empire. This is to be found in the gallery of portraits of the officers of the 8th painted by Boos at the end of the Consular period and preserved in the Musée de l'Armée.

Officer wearing social dress from the middle period of the Empire.

With this type of uniform, the Light Cavalry sabre was been replaced by a sword.

Senior Officer in around 1804, according to a set of drawings by Hoffmann.

The shako has a tall aigrette fixed on the left-hand side. The position of this ornament is unusual because it was more often than not fixed to the front of the head dress.

Officer wearing barracks dress towards 1809 by R. Knötel

Officer in town dress around 1812.

The 8th hussars: the Colonels

Uniform worn by Colonel Laborde according to a portrait preserved in the Musée de l'Armée.

In this portrait, the Colonel is wearing other foreign decorations which we have not shown here for lack of precise enough information about them. It is a head and shoulders portrait of the Colonel so we have filled in by adding the breeches used by the regiment. We do not know which sabretache he used.

Colonel Marulaz' *Croix de la Légion d'Honneur.*

Front and rear of Colonel Marulaz' sabretache.

Uniform worn by Colonel Marulaz according to a portrait by L. Rousselot. The heron plume differentiated the Colonel who was the only person to wear this type of plume. The cloth shabrack bears a double silver stripe.

BBIBLIOGRAPHY

— *L'armée française*. Planches de Lucien Rousselot
— *Carnet de la Sabretache*. Spécial hussards, année 1970
— *Soldats du temps jadis (planches)* et *Manuscrit du canonnier Hahlo* sur les uniformes de l'Empire, R. Forthoffer.
— *La cavalerie française et son harnachement,* Colonel Dugué Mac Carthy. *Editions Maloine*
— *La cavalerie au temps des chevaux.* Colonel Dugué Mac Carthy. *EPA*
— *Guide à l'usage des costumiers et artistes.* H. Malibran
— *Les Hussards*. Rigo. Série U. *Editions « Le Plumet »*
— *Histoire de la cavalerie française*. Général Suzanne
— *Les équipements militaires 1600-1870*.Tome IV Michel Pétard. *Chez l'auteur*
— *Les soldats de l'Empire*. L. & F. Funcken. *Casterman*
— *Napolenic uniforms*. J. Elting. *Mac Millan*
— *La cavalerie légère*. Commandant Bucquoy. *Jacques Grancher éditeur*
— *Fanfares et musique* Commandant Bucquoy. *Jacques Grancher éditeur*
— *Lettres de guerre*. Pierre Charrié. *Editions du Canonnier*
— *Drapeaux et étendards de la Révolution à l'Empire*. Pierre Charrié. *Copernic*
— *La cavalerie légère*. Michel Pérard et Rigo. *Histoire & Collections*.
— *Soldat et uniformes du Premier Empire*. F.-G. Hourtoulle. *Histoire & Collections*.
— *Des sabres et des épées*. Michel Pétard. *Editions du Canonnier*
— *Napoleon's soldier*. Manuscrit de Otto. G. Dempsey. *Arms and Armour press.*
— *Napoleon's army gravures*. Martinet. G. Dempsey. *Arms and Armour press.*
— Collection du Musée de l'Armée. Paris
— Collections du Musée de Nancy
— Collection du Musée de l'Emperi

ACKNOWLEDGEMENTS

We would like to thank *Rigo, Michel Pétard, Dr François-Guy Hourtoulle, M. Lapray* and *Jean-Louis Viau* and *Denis Gandilhon* for their precious help as much morale-wise as editorially. We would like to pay them the tribute which they deserve.

Design, creation, lay-out and realisation by ANDRE JOUINEAU and JEAN-MARIE MONGIN.
Computer Drawings by André JOUINEAU
© *Histoire & Collections* 2006

ISBN: 2-915239-54-1
Publish number: 2-915239

Un ouvrage édité par
HISTOIRE & COLLECTIONS
SA au capital de 182 938, 82 €
5, avenue de la République F-75541 Paris Cédex 11
▶ **N° Indigo** 0 820 888 911
0,118 € TTC / MN
Fax 01 47 00 51 11
www.histoireetcollections.fr

This book has been designed, typed, laid-out and processed by *Histoire & Collections*, fully on integrated computer equipment

Printed by Zure
Spain, European Union
April 2006